*T*o the One God Loves:

My sister — my friend

*F*rom:

Lynn

*D*ate:

March 29, 20__

Love Letters From *God*

By
Bonnie G. Schluter

www.xulonpress.com

Love Letters From God

TO

—my husband and sons who believed in me
—my brother and sisters who encouraged me
—friends whom I loved through the years
—ministers who sowed the Word in my heart
—my mother and father, now with the Lord
—my students at Victory Christian School
—Marilyn Price who reviewed and typed my letters

Truly we are a composite of the input of the people
we meet and associate with throughout our lives.

*E*SPECIALLY TO

—my mother, Sally Acosta Galjour,
who was the first to teach me the power of love,
forgiveness, and the spoken and written word.

—my sister, Rose Mary Galjour Duet
Thank you for your faith in me.
Your confidence in me encouraged me to do my best.
Your prayers kept hope alive in my heart and
surrounded me with the peace I needed.
Your fellowship with Jesus planted seeds within me
that gave birth to many of these letters.
Your enthusiastic acceptance and childlike faith
cheered me on and gave me strength.
Thank you for being a God directed,
unselfish silent partner.
Through you I dedicate this book to Jesus in you, Who
has inspired and strengthened me.
Thank you for being you and for loving me.

Love from God and me, Bonnie Galjour Schluter
1932-1991

PREFACE

It was with loving affirmation that Bonnie Schluter penned these *Love Letters from God* to encourage her sons when they left home for college and for her sisters struggling with raising families of their own.

Before she passed away in 1991, Mrs. Schluter left a loving legacy for her sons as they settled into their families and successful careers. It was her wish that these letters would touch many other hearts with God's abiding love and grace.

ABOUT THE AUTHOR

Bonnie G. Schluter was born in Larose, Louisiana. She graduated from Louisiana State University with a B.S. in Home Economics Education. In 1952, she married Robert Schluter, who is retired from the U.S. Department of Defense, Defense Contract Management Agency. The Schluters have three sons: Dr. Eric Schluter of Tulsa, Oklahoma, Dr. Marc Schluter of Bartlesville, Oklahoma, and U.S. Navy Chaplain Lt. Cmdr. Greg Schluter of Oceanside, California. They also have 6 grandchildren.

Mrs. Schluter taught high school in Tulsa and elementary school in Baton Rouge, Louisiana, and also tutored children in migrant workers education programs in Rogers, Arkansas.

You yourselves are our letter,
written on our hearts, known and read
by everybody. You show that you are
a letter from Christ, the result of our
ministry, written not with ink but with
the Spirit of the living God, not on tablets
of stone but on tablets of human hearts

—2 Corinthians 3:23 NIV

CONTENTS

BE A LIVING EPISTLE

My Child:

You have stood tall, and I have heard your voice. From the first moment you made Me the Lord of your life, My resources have been working for you. I have guided you, placed people in your path to minister and encourage you. My eye is ever looking for someone who will show himself strong in My behalf, and I have found such a one in you.

You are My chosen one! I have selected you to be My child, to fellowship with Me and to bring Me pleasure.

I would that My house be filled with sons and daughters. Go and be who you are! Walk as a living epistle, so that others may know Me through you, through your success, your peace, your calm assurance of who you are—a child of the King. Yes, you are that living epistle that I desire. In this way shall you draw others to Me.

My child, I desire that you lack nothing and you shall not want. For I am the Good Shepherd. I take care of My sheep. Rely on Me as the sheep rely on their shepherd. Let Me do it for you. Release your cares on Me. Look to Me for the answers! Seek first My Kingdom and all others things shall be added unto you. Be led by My Spirit, for this is how you are led.

Never make a decision without first consulting Me. I will lead you and guide you by My Spirit. You shall know My voice, because you fellowship with Me in My Word. Keep the lines of communication open always, and you will never be doubtful when you hear My voice. I am pleased with you, My child. Yes, I am pleased.

I am here with you now. I am always with you. I am your provision. I am your compassion. I am your wisdom. I am your intercessor. I am always on time. I am ready to do some mighty things in your life. I have always been ready. You were not prepared to receive them. Receive now the fullness of your inheritance, as a join-heir their with My Son.

Hold close to Me. Keep your focus single. Do not waver. Be single minded. Be God minded. Remember, you have not chosen Me, but I have chosen you that you should go and bring forth fruit, and that your fruit should remain; that whatsoever you shall ask Me in Jesus' name, it shall be given to you (John 15:16).

Love, God

OBEDIENT TO THE SPIRIT

My Beloved Child:

I'm talking to you daily. I'm telling you what you need to do to prepare yourself to be of service to the Kingdom of God.

One day I'll call you "loud and clear." And you will obey. Even if your mind doesn't agree, I know you will obey your spirit. How do I know? I know because I sent someone to teach you how to be led by the Spirit of God.

I have observed that you are quick to learn whatever is set before you. You are so willing to develop your mind and your spirit that you respond to whatever teaching is placed before you. Not many of My children do so. It is your diligence to excel and to conform to the standard I have placed before you that makes you so precious in My sight.

I love all of My children, for I am no respecter of persons. There is nothing too bad for Me to forgive in anyone. There is nothing anyone can do that would make Me love them less, for My love is unconditional. I truly love all of My children, but not all of My children give Me pleasure.

Some of My children turn away from Me. Some continually follow their own will instead of mine. Some hide their talents. Some waste their talents. I do not love those who do this less than I love you; but, oh, what a joy it is to have someone you love do what they are called to do! To obey is better than sacrifice.

What a joy it is to see someone you love following the right path that leads to the abundant life! What a joy it is to see someone like you, determined to be all that I have called you to be. Yes, it gives Me great pleasure to see you continually striving to follow Me in all things.

In obedience, always begin your day with Me. Devote at least an hour to Me. Pray your day, and I will plan your day so well that you will be able to perform all your duties without rushing and without effort, and you will still have time to witness for Me.

Be alert to the Spirit Who dwells within you. Listen to My voice, and you will know what to do in each and every circumstance.

Praise Me in everything. In everything give thanks!

Love, God

LET GO OF THE PAST

My Child!

Give up! Give up! Give up those hurts of the past. It's time to move on. Satan loves to have you live in the past because that renders you ineffective to live in the present—in the now.

Tell Me, child. What is it that has happened to you? Who hurt you? What hurt you? What mistakes have you made that you regret? Did what happened to you change the fact that Jesus loves you, and He died on the cross for you so you could live in heaven with Him for all eternity?

Can anything or anyone ever change that fact? You know that nothing can ever nullify what Jesus did for you on the cross. If that's true, and it is, then nothing else matters, does it?

There is nothing that can happen to you, nothing anyone can do to you that can ever change the fact that My Son, Jesus, loves you and died on the cross for you so you can gain heaven for all eternity. No one can ever take that away from you. No one!

Hold on to that thought. Put things in their proper perspective. When you do that, you'll see that being loved unconditionally, attaining salvation and the right to go to heaven is your ultimate goal. Everything else pales in comparison to that.

Even physical death cannot take heaven away from you, for then the real you—your spirit—just changes abodes. Physical death for the Christian is moving from living in the temple of the Holy Spirit, your body, to living in heaven.

I know, My child, I know. Your mind is often filled with hurtful things that have happened to you. Sometimes you even say to people, "You don't know how much it hurt me when such and such happened," and "It was so hard when this or that happened." Well,

I ask you again, does what happened to you in the past change the fact that Jesus loves you and died for you, and now you can spend eternity with Him in heaven? I don't have to wait for your answer, because I know that immediately your mind said, "No!"

Then, child, nothing else matters! Compared to eternity, all problems are nothing. Loving Me, being in My family, gaining the right to live in heaven for all eternity—that's what's important in life. If you lose that, you've lost it all. Nothing you can gain on earth can make up for that loss, and nothing can happen to you on earth that can take that away from you—Nothing!

Love, God

LOVE YOURSELF

Dear One:

I can see that you desire to know more about Me. Every day you seek Me and My ways. Unfortunately, you believe that you aren't seeking Me because you are not reading the Word as much as you think you should. You often put yourself down because of this.

Child, reading the Word does not make you a doer of the Word. There are many who read about Me and My ways, and still they are not changed by what they read. They are forgetful hearers. They deceive themselves because they are not doers of the Word (James 2:22,25). They read about Me—but they don't know Me.

If you would look within yourself and analyze what you do and why you do it, you would find more of Me—for you see, you and I are alike in so many ways. I am a giver and you are a giver.

I always give to supply a person's deepest need. When they brought a man sick of the palsy to Me, I immediately met his greatest need when I said to him, "Son, be of good cheer; thy sins be forgiven thee" (Matthew 9:2). That was his greatest need, to be forgiven. I met his spiritual need first. Then I told him, "Arise, take up your bed and walk." This met his physical need.

You have always been a giver. You give your possessions and money to people who are in need. The world focuses on this kind of giving, but I have noticed that you go further and give of yourself to all you meet. You give to everyone whose life touches yours. You daily give your time, your prayers, your love to those who are around you.

It is this type of giving that sets you apart from the world. You always give in such a way that you touch the "real" need in a person's life. Often the need you meet in a person's life isn't even recognized as a need—but you are sensitive to the needs of others.

You have so much compassion that you respond in love even to what they will need in the future. That's what prompts you to write a letter of encouragement to a friend even before discouragement sets in. That's what prompts you to send ten dollars to someone even before they have a need to pay a bill. That's what prompts you to send a gift to someone so that when it arrives three to five days later, it picks them up out of the doldrums. It is that compassion within you that does the giving.

Love, God

TOTALLY CHRIST'S

Dearest Child:

Because you are easily moved by the distresses, sufferings, wants, and infirmities of others, you show mercy to people. Your tenderness of heart allows you to overlook injuries caused by others. It allows you to treat an offender better than he may deserve. It allows forgiveness to flow from you to others. So you see, you have obeyed My Word that says, "Be merciful, as your heavenly Father is merciful." That is the beginning of being totally Christ's.

Still, you are My own. I have called you. I have nurtured you. You are in that place where I can bless you unlimitedly, because you have totally submitted yourself to Me.

It is no longer, "I can do all things through Christ who strengthens me." Now it is, "Christ does all things through me." There is a difference, you know. The first shows that you have placed your confidence in Me to work through you. The second shows that you allow Me to work through you at will, because you continuously submit yourself to Me, so much so that My desires are your desires, My will is your will, My concerns are your concerns, My goals are your goals. This is a good thing!

It isn't so much that you search to figure if your goals match up to what I want you to do. No, you have finally reached the point where My goals have become such a part of you that they are your goals, too. Where I lead, you follow. You will not be led astray because your eyes are fixed on Me.

Remember that I am the Way, the Truth, and the Light. In Me you have found your identity, your self worth, and your security. Yes, I am the Way, and I am leading you to Me, because I am your destination. The glorious fact is that as you reach Me through Jesus, you will lead many others to Me. In all humility Jesus has said, "Come unto Me, all you that labor and are heavy laden, and I will give "you rest."

I do not want you to come to Me with empty hands. It's not possessions that I want you to bring with you, but I desire that every one of My children bring many others with them into My Kingdom. Through your love and selfless generosity, that's exactly what you are doing.

Thank you for loving Me!

I love you, God

SPIRITUAL PROGRESS

My Dear Child:

My heart rejoices at the progress you are making in your spiritual walk! I can see that you are dissatisfied with yourself. You keep looking at where you are now, and you think that your progress is not enough. You have been comparing yourself to others, and you think that you fall short of the mark. But listen to Me, you do not fall short! No, indeed, you do not fall short!

Every day you move in line with My Word. Every day you set your heart and mind on doing the best you can for Me. Yes, I know sometimes you fall short of what you have determined you would do, but I do not count that as a failure as you do. Because time and time again, I see you getting up and continuing again to do the best that you can do.

It isn't who begins the race that receives the reward—it's who finishes the race who is the victor! Many, yes, many, determine to do My will, but when the first obstacle arises and they stumble, they just lie there and give up. Worse than that, some give up and go back to the life they were living.

Granted, it is true that some begin the race and finish first in a blaze of glory. This should not deter you from continuing on in the face of the obstacles you face. You see, everyone encounters obstacles. You just are not aware of what others overcome to reach the mark. It matters not to Me how many times you stumble and fall. What matters to Me is how many times you get up and keep on going!

That is what I require of you. You may never have time to finish what I have set before you. But child, if when I return you are in the process of running towards the goal that I have set before you, I will count it done. Yes, I count anything you begin with a glad and willing heart done in My name. For you see, I look on the heart, and anyone who works day in and day out with a glad and willing heart to do My will is victorious in My eyes, and they shall receive their reward.

As long as you work to fulfill your calling, when I return, I will count it done. For truly I am a rewarder of those who diligently seek Me, and I reward those who diligently set themselves to do what I have called them to do.

Continue to be the best that you can be, and KNOW that in you I am well pleased.

Love, God

FREEDOM OF CHOICE

My Child:

If you were on a leash, I would have you bound to Me in ways that you could not resist. Whenever you went astray, all I'd have to do is pull on the leash, and I could compel you to follow.

But that is not My way. No, indeed. For you, child, have been given the freedom of choice.

I love you, child. You are valuable and precious in My sight. I want only the best for you. Even before you were born, I knew you. Even then I had plans for you. To this day I have been leading you and guiding you.

I have been placing you in situations that can help you reach your greatest potential.

I have been placing people in your path who can help you and nurture you.

I remind you that you are not on a leash. If you were, you'd be tugging and straining to go your own way. If you did not tug but followed Me obediently, I would not know the true nature of your relationship with Me.

How could I know that you really loved Me if I forced you to do the things that I commanded you to do? Force should be used on the evil one. It is him whom you should overpower by strength—the strength that I have given you in the power of My Word, the power of My blood, and the power of My name.

Everything that I ask you to do, everything that I ask you to avoid, I ask for your own good and the good of all mankind. My way is to ask, not force. Your obedience, your yielding compliance to what I have called you to do, your willing abstinence from what is forbidden *must in the end be your choice.*

I did not force you to accept My Son as your Lord and Savior. I arranged everything in your life so that you would have the opportunity to receive Jesus, but in the end, you had the power to reject Him because you have the freedom to choose. And now in your Christian walk, you still have the freedom to choose. You can be what you want to be. You can follow Me and My Word, or you can go your own way. The choice is yours.

The only force I will ever use on you is the force of love. I love you.

Love, God

FAITHFUL IN LITTLE THINGS

Dearest Child:

If you knew that you were to die within the next two hours, what would you do with that time?

Would you rush here and there trying to accomplish all the big things that you had planned to do but never got to?

Or would you just go about your day doing exactly what you would be doing if you were to live another fifty years?

What would you do? Think about it. The answer you come to will be a revelation to you, and it will change your life. Yes, this can be your turning point if you'll stop and meditate on that one question.

What would you do with two more hours to live? What could you do in that amount of time that could make up for anything you had failed to do? Two hours is not a long time to redeem the time you have wasted doing worldly things.

If you feel uncomfortable with the answers to these questions, know that it is not My intention to condemn you. Quite the contrary! I want to encourage you and lift you up.

I understand, you are always looking for some big thing to do for Me. There are no big things per se. Each little deed you do is important. It is your faithfulness in those little things—in little relationships, in little decisions, in the use of whatever gifts you have received—that add up to big things.

If you do that, you will live each day, each hour, each moment as though it were your last, knowing that if you were to die, you would not change a thing. You would not have to rush to phone your mother, your father, your brother, sister, friend, or neighbor to ask them to forgive you for a wrong, because you would have taken care of that the instant a hurt or misunderstanding occurred.

My child, that is how I want you to live. I want you to be faithful in the little things. That way, you will prove your faithfulness, and it will be easier for you to remain faithful as more is given to you. And more responsibility will be given to you, because I need someone like you who hears My voice, recognizes it, and obeys it without question. You are doing a big thing in your faithfulness.

Just continue your faithfulness, for "He that is faithful in that which is least is faithful also in much" (Luke 16:10).

Love, God

CASTING YOUR CARES

My Child:

You think you're all alone. You think no one cares. "What's the use," you say. What's the use? Hush, child. Still your mind. From time to time, everyone hurts. It isn't the end of the world. You've experienced hurt before, and it has not defeated you. It will not defeat you this time.

Just turn to Me, child. Stand firm, and do not run away. You will come through this victorious. You are victorious even now, so don't be swayed by the confusion and troubles that surround you.

And don't be moved by the turmoil within you. You are not ruled by circumstances. You can change right now! Instead of reacting in fear, respond in faith! Take action! Do something! Close your senses off to the circumstances and cast all of your cares on Me. Give Me all of your burdens.

It isn't what happens to you in life that causes you to be defeated. It's what you believe about the circumstance of your defeat. Right now, in the middle of your problems, you're standing on dry ground. You'll not drown, for you're in the River of Life. Right now, in the middle of the fiery furnace, you'll not be burned, for I am with you!

Child, you're not going under, you are going over! You're going through! The circumstances around you will not defeat you! It isn't necessary for Me to change the circumstances. All you have to do is change. Refuse to quit. Refuse to run. Refuse to react in fear. Just stand firm. Stand on My Word. Have faith in Me, for I have overcome the world.

Lift your head above your problems, and view them from your position from above. For you are above, not beneath. See how small your problems are when you view them from the right perspective?

Rest in Me, child. Abide in Me. Do not for one moment forget that My strength is your strength. You, child, are sheltered in the secret place of the Most High, and you abide in the shadow of the Almighty. Stay close to Me. Drop your burdens. Drop them. Give them all to Me. Stay in My presence, and you shall overcome.

Remember that you don't have to stand in faith for something that is already yours. All you have to do is receive it. I have said, "Peace I give you, not as the world gives do I give peace. But I give you the peace that is beyond understanding."

Love, God

CALL TO MINISTER

My Child:

O, My child, how I thank you for being obedient! Because of your obedience the plans I have for you can be manifested in your life. I have a ministry for you. I have been preparing you for that ministry since the moment you were born.

I gave you every talent that you have to equip you for that ministry. Yes, I gave you the talents you'd need to do what I called you to do *before you ever chose to follow Me.* That's how much faith I have in you! That's the confidence I had that you would choose Me, and in so doing, accept the call that I have set before you to bring many children into the Kingdom of God.

Do not look to any man to open doors of opportunity for you. I myself open the doors to the places of service that I have in mind for My children. I not only open doors, but I create the place of service and plant a new tree in virgin soil. I do not need an already existent plan. No, I make My own plans.

I do not leave anything to chance in order to reach all the souls that I long to reach. I make plans, and I reveal those plans to the ones who have heard My call and accepted it. Thank you for agreeing to be a co-laborer with Me. Together we can do it!

Be prepared for the unexpected. Miracles are coming your way every day. Be alert. Don't always be looking for large, spectacular things. My children often miss a miracle because they think it is just an ordinary coincidence. There are no coincidences in life. A coincidence is simply a miracle in which I choose to remain anonymous.

Have you sat next to someone recently who gave you the opportunity to witness to them? Did a friend phone you and ask a question that opened the door for you to minister to him? Did a stranger respond to your quick and ready smile and act in love towards you? These things, My dear child, may seem ordinary, but they are not! They are supernatural interventions done in your behalf to help you grow and reach the place of maturity that you have to be in order to follow Me in all areas of your life.

Thank you for choosing Me and allowing Me to work through you in order to bring people into the Kingdom of God. You are very precious in My sight.

Love, God

GOD'S BEST PLAN FOR YOU

My Dear One:

Every time you pray, praise My holy name. Thank Me for everything in your life. Praise Me in the good times. Praise Me in the bad times. Pray consistently. Pray without ceasing!

Keep your eyes on Me. Never give up in despair because the road to Me is sometimes rocky. I am always with you to sustain you.

Some of My children travel a short, smooth path to Me. Some a short, rocky road. Others a long, long, troubled path. It doesn't matter how you arrive, or how long it takes you. All that matters is that you reach Me, and find the comfort I have to give to you.

My arms are stretched out wide to welcome and embrace you. I will protect you. Nothing can harm you when you are cradled in the bosom of the Lord!

Now, come to Me as a little child. Tell Me all the things that you are striving to achieve. Then turn those desires over to Me. Release the weight of the future to Me. Then, because your mind will not be cluttered with confusion and reasoning, you will be free.

Ask Me what would I have you do at this moment of your life. If you need wisdom, just ask for it. You have gained knowledge on your own, and that is how it should be. I do not automatically fill My children's heads with knowledge. I have given each person a mind to acquire knowledge on his or her own, but no matter how much you study and seek and strive, wisdom will not be imparted to you by your own efforts. You must ask Me for wisdom. Ask and I will give it to you.

You will not busy yourself with things of this world. You will not be lured off course in doing the thing I have called you to do by doing something else that is good, but not my first priority for you at this moment in your life.

My child, you must seek Me and learn what My master plan is for you. Do not be deceived into doing something good in My name if it keeps you from doing what is best in My name.

When you think of Me, when you follow Me, then your life will be serene. Remember, there's a River of Life flowing out of you. Release it, and you will be fulfilled!

I love you. I love you with an everlasting love that knows no bounds.

Love, God

THE POWER OF YOUR WORDS

Dearest One:

How pleased I am with the way you talk! Blessings and cursings do not come out of your mouth for you have determined in your heart to speak only good things. Therein lies the power of your witness.

People long to be around you, for they have learned from experience that no condemnation, no words of criticism, no words that belittle shall ever be directed at them from your mouth.

Oh, the human mouth! What a wellspring of goodness it can be when it is used to uplift and encourage. The mouth! What a deadly weapon it can be when the tongue lashes out with words that wound, reject, and sometimes even destroy!

There is so much power in words! The written word and the printed word can bring joy and gladness to a person's heart; or it can bring pain, grief, and sorrow.

My dearest one, if only people would learn to control their speech, there would not be so much anguish in this world, so much hurt. Too often one sentence uttered causes so much hurt and trouble that it takes hundreds of words to ease the pain and bring the relationship back to what it was before. How much easier it would have been if that one hurtful sentence had never been spoken!

Continue to set your heart on being a blessing with your words and actions.

Continue to cast down any thought that enters your mind that does not encourage and edify.

Continue to strive to be better each day. The more you practice it, the more you will accomplish it.

Never ever think that words spoken in haste or hate have to stand forever. No, those words can be nullified with My Word. If ever you slip with your tongue and cause hurt, quickly repent. If you are unable to speak healing words to that person, write healing words to them.

Think, child. Sit quietly and think. Can you recall words that have been spoken to you that have hurt you? Can you not recall words spoken to you that have blessed you? Learn to erase the hurtful words from your mind by forgiving the one who spoke them and think on the good things that have been said to you.

Look at every person you see as an opportunity for you to sow words that help them and glorify Me. And don't ever give up! Don't ever stop sowing life-giving words!

Love, God

TAKING YOUR AUTHORITY

My Child:

Why do you fret and worry? Why are you concerned with the circumstances around you? Why is there a feeling of hopelessness in you right now, a feeling that this life is too much for you, that it's too difficult to cope with the situations around you?

Yes, I know how you feel at this moment. It seems that as soon as you conquer one set of circumstances and get those working right, another set of circumstances arises that has to be conquered. In yourself sometimes you feel like giving up. You cry out to Me, "Why me, Lord? Why me?"

Child, it is not you who is being fought. It is Me in you! It isn't your plans that are being rejected. It is your fulfillment of My plans that is being rejected!

It isn't you that the world wants to hold back and smother. It is the life and light and love of God that shine from you that the world is trying to quench. When you understand that, you will no longer be moved by the circumstances around you. When you get a hold of the fact that circumstances are to be overcome in Me, you will keep your eyes on Me.

When you understand that the things of this world are temporal, while the things of the Spirit are everlasting, you will keep your eyes on Me, and victory will be yours!

You've heard lots of people say that the way to survive in this world is to live by the saying, "Don't sweat the small stuff." That is good advice, and now I say to you, child, that "it is all small stuff!" Because My Word says "nothing is too difficult for Me" (Jeremiah 32:17).

Look around at the thousands of living creatures I have created. Every one of these depends on Me for their daily food. All they have to do is gather it. Child, the birds have no concern as to where their food will come from.

So it should be with you, child. Day in and day out, year in and year out, circumstances will come rushing toward you in one way or another. But you are My child, and circumstances in the world are not to dominate you.

Therefore, take your authority to set the boundary as to how far Satan can rule over you. You can set the boundary. Rise up and resist him in Jesus' name. Tell Satan, "That's enough! You can't have my family. You can't invade my home. My life is off limits to you. My family is off limits to you." In Jesus' name, we're free!

Love, God

COUNTING YOUR BLESSINGS

My Dear Child:

Take time to count your blessings! You are focusing your eyes on what you don't have instead of what you do have. Your needs will always be evident, because it is human nature to replace one need with another as soon as one is met.

Let not your sights be set on your needs, but on Me; for when you accepted My Son you received the greatest gift, for He is the Way into all that I have. He is the Source of everything! All that He has is yours! The cost of receiving your needs met is simply to seek Me first, for then all the things you need will be added unto you.

Begin to thank Me that you have the seed of My love within you, for My love will bring you into fulfillment never before known.

Begin to thank Me that you have the seeds of My grace and mercy in you, for they will expand your joy of living.

Begin to thank Me for the seed of My compassion that has been implanted within you, for it will open to you a new world of caring.

Begin to thank Me for the seed of My light in you, for because of it you have become a beacon of hope to a lost and dying world.

Begin to rejoice for your blessings, My child, the greatest of which is that I am the I AM! And know that I'll not fail you in meeting your every need.

I'll not fail you, because I love you! I call you blessed. All that I am, you are! And all that I have is yours! Do not ever feel that your life is not worth anything, for I live big in you. You are so very precious to Me. Even if you were the only person on earth, My Son would have died just to save you.

I have created each person unique and different. No one can take your place in My master plan. You, yes, you were created to have a very special part!

Press on toward the mark you have set your eyes upon. Keep your eyes on Me. Never turn back. Remember, I am always with you, and I will cause everything you touch to prosper. You and I are a team!

Love, God

ENCOURAGEMENT FOR MINISTRY

Dear Child:

Know that perilous times will come, but I promise to slip My hand under every burden that they bring. Your burdens will be light, because you have learned to cast them on Me.

As you minister, trouble may be all around you, but it will never get in you. You shall be an oasis of peace, a refreshing river of contentment that many will drink from. There is truly a River of Life flowing out of you that I supply. You shall never exhaust My water of life that springs from the river. The more you give, the more will be given to you.

Go, My child, and do the work I've called you to. The time is now. As you have prepared the way in your spirit, soul, and body for Me to do a mighty work in you, I have prepared the way for you to go into the world and preach the gospel to every living creature.

Go, My child, and preach everywhere I have called you to go, and I will work with you confirming My Word with signs that will follow.

You are not alone in your ministry; together we will do what I've called you to do!

I will never leave you. Yea, though you walk through the valley of the shadow of death, fear no evil, for I am with you: My rod and My staff, they are there to comfort you.

My child, I have prepared a table for you in the presence of your enemies. I have anointed your head with oil. Goodness and mercy shall follow you all the days of your life, and you shall dwell in the house of the Lord forever.

This is my promise, if you keep your eyes on Me. Don't look to the right nor to the left! Keep your eyes fixed on Me and My Word, and you will see success. You have become an overcomer.

Circumstances will not rule your life anymore, because you are submitted to Me and you resist the devil in the name of Jesus.

Trust in Me, child. I am the guarantor of your ministry. I am your God, your protector. When you call upon Me, I will answer. I will not leave you alone. I will be with you in trouble. I will rescue you. I will satisfy you with a full life, because you love Me and keep My commandments.

Love, God

COMFORT IN THE MIDST OF DIFFICULTIES

My Child:

You are not alone, for I am always with you! There is no sadness, no depression, no discouragement, no loneliness that can engulf you and take you captive if you remember that I am always with you.

Are you in a desperate financial situation? Fear not. I am with you.

Are you feeling lost and alone? Fear not. I am with you.

Is your body hurt and do you feel broken? Fear not. I am with you.

Oh, child, if you'd just remember to talk to Me daily! What a difference it would make in your life! I have said in My Word, "I am with you always." Remember that. Do not ignore Me.

When you wake up in the morning, acknowledge My presence by saying, "Good morning, Lord. Thank You for this beautiful day." Talk to Me often during the day, and when you go to bed at night, remember to talk to Me again. Say, "Father, I thank You that You are ever with me and that the angels of the Lord encamp around about me, giving me protection all through the night."

Oh, My child! Just call out to Me, and I will answer, for I desire for you to live the abundant life. I desire for you to live in peace, in joy, and in prosperity. I desire for you to be free—spirit, soul, and body. I desire for you to be healed. I desire for you to be prosperous, and you are prosperous for I have paid the price so that you could obtain all of these things.

All these things are now yours in the Spirit. All that remains for you is to receive these blessings in My name. In the name of

Jesus, you're free! You're delivered from the kingdom of darkness into the Kingdom of Light.

Do not listen to the world and its problems. Listen to Me and My Word. Do not meditate on everything wrong in your life. Put your confidence in Me, child. Believe! For I will stand before you and protect you. I am your hiding place. Just turn to Me, and believe that what I've said in My Word, for I am well able and willing to perform.

I long to be Lord of your life. Just release to Me all your cares and burdens. Let go. Loose them, and let them go.

Refuse to dwell on the bad. Begin at once to meditate on the positive answers contained in My Word. Keep My Word ever before you. Keep it on your lips, for you overcome by the blood of the Lamb and the word of your testimony.

Love, God

GOD'D LOVE FOR YOU

My Beloved Child:

You think I do not love you! My child! My child! My child! If I were to react in the measure that you react, it would be I who would think that you do not love Me.

"Oh," you protest! "Father, I do love You! I love You with every fiber of my being." But I say to you, if that is true, then why don't you trust Me? If you love Me, why don't you believe Me? I have told you over and over in My Word that I love you, and I have demonstrated by My actions that I love you.

My dear child, didn't I send My only Son to die on the cross for you? Why was I willing to do that for you? Because I love you so much that I wanted to have fellowship with you again.

The thought of going through eternity without having fellowship with you was too painful for Me to bear, so I devised a plan, and My Son graciously consented to execute that plan.

You accept Jesus' love. You believe that He loves you because He was willing to die for you, and you are so right. For greater love hath no man than He lay His life down for another.

And where was I in this plan? I was the designer, the architect, the Master Blueprint of this plan of redemption. I knew that there was no way that I could regain you and your love and fellowship without sacrificing My only Son, Jesus.

Jesus had a choice. He could have refused to die for you. But I had a choice too. I could have refused to even present the plan of salvation to Jesus. I could have stopped it before it began.

You see, it is I, your Father. It is I, El Shaddai, the Almighty, the All-Powerful One, who gave Jesus the opportunity to die for you. Without that opportunity, He could not have said "yes," for I am the Person in the Godhead who makes the plans. Jesus executes the plans, and the Holy Spirit guides and empowers them.

Oh, yes, I know you don't understand the mystery of the Godhead that is hidden in Me. It isn't necessary that you understand. All you have to do is *believe and receive.*

How we rejoiced in heaven when you made Jesus the Lord of your life! How happy we were that you joined Our family! And now, how each morning I await you wakening so that you can fellowship with Me! How I wait for you to receive and open and use the gifts that I have already given you!

Love, God

MY GREATEST GIFT TO YOU IS LOVE

My Dear Child:

My love for you never changes. I loved you when you were in sin. I loved you when you made Jesus the Lord of your life. I love you now. I will always love you.

Receive My love, and you will be free of the fear that has been tormenting you. You will no longer be tormented with thoughts that I will reject you. For you see, child, perfect love casts out fear, and My love for you is perfect.

I love you. I do love you. I am pleased with you. You are so very dear to Me. I accept the love you have given Me. Do not offend Me, child, by refusing My love. I hold it out to you in tenderness as your heavenly Father. The greatest gift I have to give you is My love. Accept it. Cherish it. Walk in it. Give it freely to others. Receive it unlimitedly.

Accepting My love is not a one-time happening. The more you receive it, the more you increase your capacity to continue receiving it. And then, recognize that the more you have, the more you can give. The more you give, the more you can be a blessing to others. And that's what you were born to be—a blessing.

Go forth now in the name of Jesus, and bless others with My love that has been shed abroad in your heart. Allow it to spill over into the heart of everyone you meet. Allow your family to be beneficiaries of the love I heap upon you.

Because of My love, always begin your day with Me. Turn to Me with all of your joys. Turn to Me with all of your sorrows. Give everything to Me. I long to help you. I long to carry your burdens. I long to share your joys. You are My child, and I am your Father. I delight in you and want you to spend time fellow-shipping with Me.

The things that sound simple to do are simple when you abide in Me. Whenever you find yourself unable to "let go," you can be sure that you have drawn away from Me. You should be aware of My presence at all times, for I am with you always.

Being aware of My presence is being aware of all of the ways that I have influenced your life. Keep your eyes on Me, and you will not only love to live, but you will live to love!

Love, God

WALK IN LOVE

Dear One:

My love is flowing through you with ever increasing frequency. You experience this often now because you have torn down most of the barriers that keep Me out. The inner peace and joy that you will experience when you give yourself to Me completely will be indescribable, but very evident to all who see you and know you.

I am in loving control working things out for your good. The most important thing you have to do right now is stay in love. You must not violate the Love Commandment.

As long as you stay in love, as long as you walk the love walk with each member of your family, with the people you work with, and with each and every person you meet, fear cannot come in, because perfect love casts out all fear. Walking in love requires that you walk free from fear.

Love is the root of everything we have to do. It's the bottom line. It's not something you choose to do or not to do. It is My commandment, and it is so easy to fulfill when you remember that each and every person you meet either has Me residing in them or they have the potential of having Me reside in them.

Consider this every time you meet someone. Consider that you are face to face with Me. What would you say to Me? How would you treat Me? Then treat them accordingly, for as long as you do good to the least of My brethren, you've done it to Me.

Always remember that walking in love puts you in the position of being a giver, and when you give, you put yourself in a position where I can bless you. That is My desire, to bless you. Be a blessing to everyone you meet, and I will bless you unlimitedly.

To demonstrate My love, I urge you to approach My throne of grace boldly. I am your Father. I will not refuse you. I will make it possible for you to walk in love. Come to Me, and I will never turn you away.

My love for you is revealed in what I have done for you—your redemption. My love looked past all sin, iniquity, and wickedness. I long to reveal to you the breadth, length, depth, and width of My love. I have loved you with an everlasting love. Therefore, with loving-kindness have I drawn thee.

Because I love, I long to bring you into My family right now.

Love, God

A CHRIST-LIKE WITNESS

Dear Child:

Lifting your hands, you sing hallelujah. Sing hallelujah, lifting your hands! I am so happy that you are free in Me. I am so happy that you are not ashamed to praise Me.

My child, I want you to know that I have never been ashamed of you. Yes, I know that there were times in the past you have not stood up for Me. When someone has taken My name in vain, you have felt pain within your heart; yet you did not speak up and defend Me for fear of hurting someone, for fear that they would think that you are not a nice Christian.

But no more! Truly today you are on My side—spirit, soul, and body. You are a witness to the power that is within you as a child of God. Many people have come into the Kingdom of God, and many more will come because your life is a good example of the good things that I can bring into My children's lives. I would that all of Mine were as diligent as you in overcoming the flesh.

Never forget that I inhabit your praises. Continue to praise Me in all things, and you will not only be a witness to others but you will be an overcomer in all areas of your life.

Always remember that I love you very much. I loved you before you were born. I love you now. I'll always love you!

In My love there is no need to fret and worry. Haven't I said that I would never leave you nor forsake you? I am here. I am with you. You are not alone. Just be quiet. Listen to your heart. Still your mind. Close your eyes, and focus on Me and My love for you. Mind, be still in Jesus' name.

Take a deep breath, and breathe in My love for you. In you I live and move and have My being. Don't you realize that I am with you? I am here, ready and willing to help you at all times.

Before you call, I answer. What is it you would have Me do for you right now? What is it that is consuming your thoughts? Is the problem bigger than Me? Is anything bigger than Me? No! A thousand times no!

I am El Shaddai! I am all sufficient! I am your mother, your father, your nurse, your friend, the supreme Provider of everything that you need in life.

Peace be to you, My child.

Love, God

COMMUNING WITH JESUS

My Dear Child:

What a joy it is to fellowship with you! I wait for you to awaken each day so that you can talk to Me. My child, you don't have to be formal when you talk to Me. You don't have to be continually quoting Scriptures, nor do you have to speak poetically.

No, all you have to do is talk to Me as you would talk to a friend, as you would talk to your father and mother.

I am always ready to listen to you. Is there anything that's bothering you? Tell Me about it. I want to help. Are there any hurts in your life? Release them to Me right now. I am more than able to heal and comfort you.

I want you to come to Me with all of your needs. I never tire of listening to you, even if the only time you talk to Me is to tell Me your troubles. But, My child, think! Did anything good happen to you lately? Did anything good happen to you today? Tell Me about it. Share your joys with Me. I am willing and able to help you by standing with you when you share your hurts and disappointments, but I also enjoy sharing your successes.

It makes Me so happy when you come running to Me to tell Me good news. It thrills My heart to know that you want to share something good from your life with Me.

We are partners in this Christian life.

When you hurt, I hurt. When you are happy, it makes Me happy. Come, My child. Come. Don't ever feel that you cannot come boldly to Me when you need help. It is My desire to always be available to help you. Run to Me when you are in trouble, but also run to Me with your happy times and your successes.

Always come running to Me and tell Me the good news in your life. It will not only bless Me, but it will get you in the habit of sharing the good, of speaking good reports. The more you do this, the more the bad reports will diminish in your life.

Publish the good things that are happening to you, and more good will happen. Just watch and see if this isn't so!

Love, God

PRESSING ONWARD IN CHRIST

Dearest One:

My child! My child! What are you doing with that basket covering your head? Why are you hiding your light? Lift up! Lift up! I say, lift yourself up and remove all of the shackles that try to bind you to this earth and all of its trappings.

Long ages ago I called you to a new life in Me. You have grown in Me, and I am pleased with your progress. But oh, if you'd know the heights you could have attained in these past few years, yes, even these past few months, you would not be satisfied with where you are right now.

The time is short. I need you. There are so few who are willing to walk in perfect love—forsaking self, things, and all others for Me.

I looked a long time to find you. There was much joy in heaven when you entered the Kingdom because we know that you are the key to bringing your whole family in. Your family is doing and will do many exploits in My name.

But what about you? Are you satisfied with the harvest you have reaped in your life? Are you satisfied with the harvest you have reaped for My Kingdom?

Lift yourself up and venture forth boldly in My name. Travel the unknown paths that I set before you. You will not be alone. I am with you. Just go in My name, and together we will get the job done. Even if no one else is willing, you be willing.

Guard against discouragement. That's Satan's tool to hinder you and My work in you and through you. My work will go on. My work must go on. If it does not, many will fall into the pit, into the everlasting lake of fire.

My plan is that all would come into the fullness and knowledge of Me. My Spirit is there to help you. My Father and I await the appointed time for My return. Until then, you must be about the work I have called you to do. Then many will come into My family, and great will be your reward in heaven.

My child, I beseech you, do not hesitate to take these words to heart. I urge you, do not procrastinate, determine to become active. Decide daily to be involved in personal behavior and attitudes that will have everlasting positive effects on My Kingdom.

Love, God

GROWING UP IN CHRIST

My Dear Child:

Springtime is now in your heart, because My Holy Spirit dwells in you! Now you need never be alone again. No more will you look to your own understanding to solve your problems, because I abide in you.

Each day you will need to release your problems, fears, doubts, and discouragements to Me. When you do this, a little of you will die. This death of self will become a never ending process. Because you empty yourself, the result will be more of Christ within you. That will enable Him to shine through you. The light of the Godhead will shine through you like a beacon that will make you My witness. I am asking you to "Be" not "Do." Be Christ like through the emptying of self.

My child, and you are My child, I need you. I need your freely given love. No one can give this to Me but you.

Do you need Me? Have you come to the point in your life where you realize that life without Me is dead? Remember above all things that I wish that you should prosper and be in health, even as your soul prospers.

It is so easy to have abundant life, peace, and prosperity. Why do My children make it such a difficult task? Why do you hold back? Do you think that I would ever do anything to hurt or embarrass you? I would not.

I have abundant gifts for you, but I will not force them on you. You must accept them. You have accepted them. You accepted them when you proclaimed Jesus Christ as your Lord and Savior. You accepted them when you asked for the baptism of the Holy Spirit.

You now possess all My gifts. But, My child, you have not opened a single one of them. Each day that you live without using My gifts is wasted time. Are you content to be happy with Me someday in heaven? Or do you want the abundant life that is available to you now? All you need do is open your gifts. No one can do it for you. You must do it yourself!

Because you are a maturing Christian, not only do you need My gifts, but you must be fed by the Word. I invite you to come to Me and taste how good life can be. In Me is security! In Me is peace! In Me is joy! In Me is prosperity! These are the gifts I have for you.

I love you, child. Oh, how I love you!

Love, God

PEACE BE STILL — IN MY WILL

My Child:

Be still! Do not meditate on the problem. Do not replay the words said to you that have inflicted hurt upon you. Be still and know that I am God and that I am well able and willing to take care of you.

What is it that you need right now? Come to Me. Ask of Me, and I will give you all things that pertain to life and godliness. I will give you new strength. I will give you new joy.

Peace, be still! I have heard your heart's cry. I am here. Just be still. Keep your mind stayed on Me and My Word, and nothing shall harm you for I have you cradled in My arms. I cover you with feathers.

You are My child. I am your Father. I care for you. Just run to Me in your time of trouble. Don't run from Me. In Me there is refuge. In Me there is hope. In Me there is deliverance. In Me there is comfort, strength, and joy.

Peace, My child. Peace be still and know that I am God.

When you have peace, you will not be easily discouraged. I can create within you the right desires, giving you My will, My plan, My purpose for your life. That's where real peace is found.

Don't allow fear to hold you back. Because you are diligent in doing what I've called you to do, I will reveal more of My plan for your life. All you have to do is seek Me and ask Me. I will tell you what to do. I do not withhold My will from My children. Some of My children just do not hear when I speak to them because their minds are so preoccupied with other things. Some hear, but they do not listen or they reason that it is not Me speaking to them. Some listen, but they do not act. It takes all three to succeed. You must hear what I am saying. You must listen to the directions I am giving. Then you must act on the knowledge you have received.

Do not compare yourself to the world. You cannot afford that comparison. Do not compare yourself to others. Compare yourself with Me and My Word. Find in My Word who you are and what I want you to be. Delight yourself in Me. Set your goal, and then take off after it. Don't stop! Don't waver! Above all, don't quit! You will succeed because all things are possible in Me and to them who believe and act on what they believe.

Love, God

GIFT OF LAUGHTER

My Precious, Merry Child:

You have done well. You have sown the proper seeds in the proper way at the proper time. My dear beloved child, I am pleased. I am pleased!

I am pleased that you allow the eternal joy that resides in you to bubble out in unrestrained laughter.

The joy within you rises to your countenance in a ready smile. It twinkles in your eyes, finds expression in your ever moving hands, and comes out of your mouth with an explosion of breath that produces the happy, lyrical sound of laughter.

Your laughter is contagious. Your honest, spontaneous laugh changes the atmosphere in a room and causes others to automatically join in the laughter.

Your laughter is therapy. It releases tension and makes people feel at ease in your presence. Your laughter is healing. Self-pity, loneliness, and depression can't stay in the presence of your laughter. Truly a merry heart doeth good like a medicine.

Do you realize that laughter is a vocal expression of joy that is peculiar to man? Birds express happiness by singing. Cats will purr. Dogs will wag their tails to express their love and joy, but only humans have the ability to express joy by laughing.

Laughter is one of My gifts to the human race, and you, dear one, have tapped into its power.

Thank you, dear child, for allowing joy to flow from you; happiness to show through you; and love to glow in you. Take that gift of laughter and spread it everywhere you go, for truly the joy of the Lord is your strength.

As My child, remember that the joy of the Lord is your strength.

With your humor and joy, it delights My heart that you are in My family. Heaven will be a happier place because you will someday be here.

Lovingly, God

FAITH

Dear Child:

Faith is the key that unlocks the door to My storehouse. With faith, you can tap into My supply. With faith, your sins can draw on My forgiveness. Your sickness can draw on My healing power. Your poverty can draw on My prosperity. Your faith can link your impossibility with My possibility.

You begin to do all you can in yourself, and I will perform through you. Your acts and feats will astound you and amaze the world. Decide to do, and you will!

You and I are a team!

As part of My team, I ask you to be what I've called you to be. Don't go back to your old ways, for I have shut the door on your past, so no man can open that door.

When I shut the door on your past, I opened other doors. With your key of faith in hand, recognize that I have set before you choices, some lead to eternal life, others lead to eternal damnation—life and death, blessings and cursings, power and weakness, prosperity and poverty, health and sickness, success and failure.

Because you have faith in My promise to be with you, you choose the course you will take. You decide what needs to be done—then do it!

My child, I am coming soon; and I have chosen you to help prepare the way for Me. Just as John the Baptist was called to prepare the way for My Son's first coming, you have been called to prepare the way for His second coming.

Heed My call. With the key of faith, take up your cross and follow Me. Know that I am in you, and I am with you all the days of your life.

A person of faith understands the danger in the phrase, "I'll do something for God someday, but I just don't have time today."

When you consistently put off performing exploits for Me, nothing ever gets done. As I have said, that is one of the major problems in the world today. You will never intentionally disobey or neglect My requirements, but that is what you are doing when you put off this responsibility.

Don't let the devil take advantage of you in this respect. Take your place and stand on your rights as a child of faith—and the devil will turn and flee from you.

Love, God

VESSEL OF LOVE

My Dear Child:

My love is flowing like a mighty river. It's flowing in and through My people. As you let it flow through you, it cleanses all of your impurities so that you can be a clean vessel kept for the Master's use.

My love will fill you up and saturate your very being until it overflows from you onto others.

My dear one, go forward, and allow My love to flow through you to the others who come into your life. When you do this, those people will be touched by the overflow of your river of love.

It is love that will make those people receptive to My Word, and it is My Word that will bring them life, and life more abundant.

So long ago I called you to new life in Me. When you accepted My call, you became submerged in My river of love, and now you have emerged as a vessel of love.

I will lead you by an inward witness. Learn to follow that inward witness in all areas of your life, and you will be successful in all that you do. Go forth, My child, in the power and might of the Holy Spirit. Be that living epistle that others will read. Be not conformed to this world, but be transformed by the renewing of your mind. When you do that, you will think what God thinks. You will fellowship with the Father, and you will bring Me pleasure, for that is why you were created—to bring Me pleasure.

Keep on moving toward the goal that I have set before you. No, it isn't easy. I know that. That's why I have given you My Word for instruction and direction. I have sent the Holy Spirit to comfort you and empower you. You are not alone. I am with you. Together we will make it.

Don't forget, I am not off in a far distant land. I am not off and high up on a pedestal. I am not untouchable. I am a Spirit, and I reside in you, a vessel of love. As you walk more and more in My light, life, and love, you will become more and more conformed to My image. For this is what you were predestined to be—My son or daughter, a join their with Jesus Christ, My Son, who is led by the Holy Spirit.

Love, God

GOD'S REWARDS

My Dear, Precious Child:

You have given much, and much has been required of you. Sometimes it seems that the more you give of yourself, the more people require of you. As you give, people are not aware of your motive, but I am well aware that you stretch yourself to the outer limits of human endurance because you want to please Me.

Every job you undertake, you do it well. Yes, I know, child, there are many people who are appreciated and rewarded financially who have not toiled the long hours that you have. They have not paid the price that you have to serve Me. You have given your all, and the world has not recognized it.

Man has put you on the same level as other people. They have taken you for granted, but child, I have not! I see, and I know what goes into the final product, and you shall have your reward.

You are doing what I called you to do, and I shall repay you. Your harvest is at hand. Never fail to turn to Me in your hour of despair. Never fail to turn to Me in your hour of joy.

I want you to come to Me with every thought you have, every problem you have, every joy you have. I am interested in you. I love you. Come to Me, and your life will be fulfilled. In Me you will find life, and life more abundant.

Through Me your mistakes can be turned around for your good. I am a forgiving Father. I don't want you to live in the past and dwell on your failures. No, child, that is not My desire for you. I desire that you climb higher and higher in Me. When you make a mistake, all you have to do is repent, pick yourself up, and keep on moving in My direction.

Never fail to turn to Me—ever! Never fail to turn to Me in your hour of despair. Never fail to turn to Me in your hour of joy. I want you to come to Me with every thought you have, every problem you have, every joy you have, every question you have. I am interested in you. I love you. Come to Me, and your life will be fulfilled. In Me you will find life, and life more abundant.

Love, God

CALLED TO WIN

My Dear Child:

Press on! If you're down, pick yourself up and get back in the race! All is not lost. Yes, I know it looks like you have made so many mistakes that it is impossible to ever get back on the right track, but you can! I promise. You see, nothing is impossible with Me. Therefore, nothing is impossible with you when you allow My Word and My ability and My power to transform you into a winner. That's what I have called you to be—a winner! Yes, that is your calling in this life and in the next. You are to be a winner!

So what does a winner do? Does a winner win each and every time in each and every contest he or she enters? Has the heavy-weight boxing champion of the world never tasted defeat? Have the Super Bowl winners ever lost a game? Has the holder of the title of the fastest miler won every race he has ever entered? You know that there is no one, not one, except Me, who has never tasted defeat.

Why then do you expect never to make a mistake, never to have a setback? What separates the champ from the loser? Is it not the fact that because you seek Me first, all things shall be added to you?

So, I wait. Yes, I sit and wait for you to do that seeking. I expect you to do what you know you need to do. That still small voice inside you that nudges you to do right, is Me talking to you.

"Turn Me loose," says this Spirit. "Turn me loose to do what should be done in your life. I will lead you on the course that will be the winning course—the path of righteousness."

Do you realize, My dear child, that residing in you is the potential to be a winner? The Greater One indwells you. All of My attributes reside in your spirit. These are potentially yours. I have declared, "I will walk in you. I will live in you. I will be your God, and you will be My people."

The champion keeps on. Setbacks do not devastate him or her. They just spur the champion on to work harder.

Does a winner go it alone in his fight to win? No, he gets the best trainer he can find, and he trusts those professionals to help. The trainer maps out a training program. He sets the course, then the athlete follows that course. My child, you do the same.

Lovingly, God

DELIVERANCE

My Precious Child:

I have seen you, My child. Yes, I have seen you. I have seen you beaten down. I have seen you hurt. I have seen you crying in the depths of despair. I have seen you, and I have been with you. My child, I have never left your side.

Precious one, Jesus bore all of your griefs—every one of them. None of them are yours—not now—not ever. Refuse them in Jesus' name!

As My Son hung on the cross with all of the sins, grief, and diseases of all mankind, I had to turn My back on Him. I could not bear to look at Him, and I cannot bear to look at you and see you wounded and hurt. Oh, My precious child, arise! Stand up! In Jesus' name, stand up and cast your cares and burdens on Me. They are not yours.

Satan, I rebuke you. Take your hands off of My precious child. Take your hands off of My child!

In My Son's name oppression shall go! In My Son's name, discouragement must go! Fear must go—in My Son's name. Loneliness must go in My Son's name! Poverty must go in My Son's name. Confusion must go in My Son's name! You are set free!

Now, lift up those hands that hang down. Lift up your voice now still and shout the victory. Yes, shout! "In the name of Jesus I have victory. I am free! Jesus has set me free!" Confess it with your mouth, "In the name of Jesus, I am free!"

My child, now you are seated in heavenly places with My Son, Jesus, and *all* things are under your feet. Satan is under your feet. He has no dominion over you.

My child, I have called you. You are My own. I have given you Jesus' name. I have given you My Word. I have given you My armor. I have left you My peace. I have called intercessors to stand in the gap for you.

My child, I have put on you the garment of praise. I have poured on you the oil of gladness. You are My child, and I am your Father. I have made all provision for you. You are a joint heir with My Son, Jesus, and you are free. In Jesus' name, you can accept your freedom!

And now, My precious child, I fill you anew with love and compassion. I cover you with the precious blood of Jesus Christ! I cover you with the blood, and you are protected from all the fiery darts of the enemy. My child, you're free. I proclaim it!

Love, God

PEACE

Dear Child:

I love you so very much. I want My love to become so real to you that you are aware of it at all times.

Before you were, I loved you. I love you now. My love for you has never ceased. It has never diminished, and it never will, because I love you with an everlasting love that no one can take away.

At this moment, My peace is enveloping you. Close your eyes, breathe deeply, and know that My peace is in you. My peace is around you. My peace is flooding through every cell, every organ, every nerve in your body. You are at peace, and I am with you.

Confusion, tension, and hate have to go. They aren't a part of your life anymore. No, you have chosen the higher life, and the higher life is a life of peace and contentment.

Right now, cast all of your cares and burdens upon Me. You were not created to carry unnecessary burdens. You were created for My pleasure. You were created to fellowship with Me.

Oh, how I long to just sit and talk to you. To listen to you. For you to tell Me what good things have happened to you today.

Are you reading this letter yourself? Rejoice that you have eyes to see and a mind that comprehends.

Are you holding this letter in your hands? Then rejoice for the fingers that are able to hold, to touch, to feel.

Rejoice, and again I say rejoice! When you rejoice in Me, you send praise up to My throne room and the enemy is stilled.

You need not cry, "Help," for before you call, I answer. All you need do is begin to rejoice and praise and know that I am with you, and I will never leave you.

When things come against you, the faith that I have given you will rise up like a tidal wave and overcome any situation that comes up against you.

Always remember that My Son gave His life for you. He took all sin, sickness, and disease upon Himself so that you would not have to pay the price. The price is paid in full. I bought and paid for you with His precious blood. His light shines through you and dispels the darkness around you.

Don't let the devil take advantage of you. Take your place and stand on your rights in Me, and the devil will have to flee.

Always remember that I love you with an everlasting love that no one can take away.

Love, God

VICTORY IN WARFARE

Oh, My Child, My Dear Child:

You have been fighting so many battles lately. It seems like there is never an end to your battles. You pray for this person and that person. You are always ready, willing, and able to stand in the gap for someone, to comfort them, to encourage them, to pray for them. I appreciate your diligence. You are truly a good soldier. Now I want you to act like one!

There comes a time in every battle when you must pull back, to regroup, to plan your strategy, to rest, to renew your strength. Now is that time. Pull back! Pull back! Pull away from the battle. Rest! Rest physically, and rest in Me! When you pull back, others will go in to fight for you, for I have called many to pray and intercede for you and every situation you're involved in. I intercede for you daily. You are not alone!

Cast your cares on Me. *All* of them. They are not yours. Let Me carry your burdens. You were not created to carry burdens.

I want to help you, but so often you won't allow Me to. You keep on wanting to do it all yourself. You have seen in the natural that if you do not do things, they don't get done. Therefore, it's understandable that you would think that you have to do it all yourself in the spiritual realm. But this is not so. I am your armor. I am your shield. I am your comforter, and I am here, ready and willing to help you.

Just trust Me. Let go. Release those cares and burdens. Seek Me. Praise Me. Worship Me. Use the authority I have given you in My name, and above all, walk in love.

When you walk in love, you fulfill all of the commandments, for they are based on love. My child, I want you to know Me and My Word. Claim the promises I have given you. My Spirit will guide you into all truth.

Daily I hold open a door that leads to abundant life. I am waiting for you to walk through that door. I love you. I love you with a love that knows no bounds. Continue to be a witness to that love, and together we will bring more people into My Kingdom.

Love, God

MATURING SPIRITUALLY

My Child:

Walk softly. Talk softly. Be what I've called you to be! I am praying for you, interceding for you, so that you can have the manifestation of those things in your life; so that your outward appearance will show the world the beautiful you that is inside. And it is happening!

Every day you draw closer and closer to perfection. Every day the external you gives evidence to those around you that the internal you, the inner person, the real you, is complete and entire and perfect in Me. Soon, very soon, everyone will see you as I see you—a pure child of God with a heart full of love and compassion and a deep desire to be a blessing to everyone you meet.

Why do you listen to thoughts that come into your head that say you are less than you are? Those thoughts are not from Me. I tell you to cast them down in My Son's name. Whatsoever a man thinketh in his heart, so is he. Think of the good things that are in you. Don't be concerned if the outward you misses it sometimes.

Don't be concerned if some of your old habits are still attached to you. They cannot dominate you anymore. As you seek Me and fill yourself with the pure, uncompromised Word of God, all of those worldly things that seem to pull you down will diminish and drop away.

Believe Me when I say this—don't dwell on what you were. Don't be overly influenced by outward signs. Just fix your eyes on Me.

You're determined to show the world that you are brand new inside—and you are brand new inside. People see you, and they know that I dwell within you. Many people are being drawn to Me, because they have witnessed and are witnessing the change

81

in you. Yes, people are reading you every day. You are My letter to the world.

Thank you, My child, for being all that I've called you to be. Hold close to Me, and you will climb higher and higher in Me.

I love you. I love you so very much. Never ever forget!

Love, God

POWER OF PRAISE

Dear One:

Praise stills the enemy! In the days of old, I did not commission the mightiest warriors to go before the army into battle. No, I commissioned praisers to be on the front lines. Praise stills the enemy. Praise pushes the enemy back. When you praise Me unashamedly, you create a force that cannot be arrested.

My child, every time you praise Me, you are putting the force of joy into effect, and that's a force that cannot be denied. There are times when the best of My children find it hard to grasp how powerful genuine praise is. They fail to realize that joy is a force to be reckoned with. That is why the joy of the Lord is their strength.

Don't allow your natural mind to reason, "How can something as simple as joy and praise deliver me?" There is only one answer to that question—it can and it does! What better proof do you need? I said that it would and it will! All you have to do is, do it! You don't even have to buy into the idea at first. Just try it.

Make a sacrifice of praise to Me. Release the force of joy and let the results benefit your life at this very moment. Let the attitude of joyful praise overwhelm your heart and mind and then let it pour out of you.

As part of this exercise in praise, I want you to laugh at the devil. Laugh at him for all you're worth! When he tries to make you feel foolish because you are praising Me, laugh at him! Because he knows all about the undeniable power of praise. Every time you obey Satan by keeping your mouth shut and refusing to praise Me, you are giving him authority to defeat you. That is a serious but true charge. Don't allow your fear to make you silent and keep your mouth shut.

Rise up! Take your place before My army. Take your place on the front lines. Your assignment in this war is to be a praiser. A praiser! Praise Me, your God, your Deliverer, the Possessor of heaven and earth. I want you on the front lines of My army, because that's where the praisers are. They lead the battle. Take your place right now!

Love, God

ENCOURAGEMENT

Dear Child:

Oh, how I glory in the stand that you have taken for Me. I look each day to see the progress you have made toward becoming more and more like Me, and I rejoice.

The more your eye becomes single and focused on Me, the less hold the trappings of the world have on you. I am refining you; I am polishing you like a diamond. And I await the day when everything you do and say, be it large or small, will be done and said to My glory.

You are My child, and in you I am well pleased. I have seen you increase in wisdom, in stature, and in favor with your fellow believers.

Because you are My child, you are not living your life alone. I can promise you, you are not going to fail. You have not come to the end of your spiritual resources. I am your Resource! I am the Source to meet all needs of your spirit, your body, and your mind.

If there is any lack in your life, it is because you have been seeking for prosperity in the wrong places. You have excluded Me from your life. The only solution for this neglect is to turn your eyes on Me and find your life solutions. Call unto Me, and I will answer. I will not ignore your cry for help. Don't be afraid, for I am with you, and I will continue to be at your side.

You should have the confidence that My eyes are ever upon you. I watch over all the plans and paths of the righteous. There is not a step you take that I don't know about. Minute by minute I bless you with favor. I protect you going in and coming out with the shield of love. Nothing can harm you as long as you keep your eyes focused on Me and My Word.

In the name of Jesus be free! Be free from unreasonable fear. Be free from oppression. Be free from all that would sadden your life. These are the benefits of the single eye focused on Me.

Love, God

STABILITY IN CHRIST

Dearest Child:

How happy I am that you are in My family! You are such a vital part. Just as the heavens tell of My glory, your life bears witness that I am your God and that I am a good God.

The sun, the moon, and the stars are a silent witness of My power, My love, My laws, and My unchangeableness. You can chart your life by My laws, because they are pure, eternal, and just.

Farmers plant their crops according to the position of the sun in the heavens to take advantage of the best weather.

Sailors plot their course over the seas by the stars that day in and day out behave according to the laws that I have set forth.

Without a word, the sun and moon give information to people who observe their reliable, never-changing, and persistent behavior.

One always knows what the sun will do; it is not fickle. It was created to conform to My laws, and My laws are perfect. They protect you and make you wise. They give you joy and light. They bring prosperity to all who obey them. So it is more and more with you, child.

Without a word or sound, the message that I am the door through which people must enter into eternal life goes forth from you day in and day out.

Yet, sometimes you let yourself be deceived into believing that you are not important to the Body of Christ. So often, you begin to think that you are a failure, that you are not pleasing Me.

My child, I remember when you asked Me to shine a light on all of your faults so you could be aware of them and change them.

I remember your request for Me to cleanse you from anything that is not pleasing to Me. You ask Me for My help so that you can change anything in you that does not glorify Me.

I am also aware that when the change isn't immediate, when you are not perfected right away, you become discouraged and think that you are not being a good witness for Me. This must stop! Your heart is tender toward Me, and as long as you put Me first place in your life, *you will not fail* because there is no failure in Me.

Just continue to be who you are, My child, who has a deep compassion to help others. Then just as the heavens silently tell of My glory, so will you!

I love you, child. Don't ever forget that!

Love, God

EDIFICATION

Dear Child:

All of My children are in need of constant uplifting. Why does it bother you that you can say things to uplift others, yet you cannot uplift yourself? Don't you realize that this is all according to My plan? If each of you could fulfill his own needs, you would become independent, and you would not need each other.

Always remember that you are all members of one body. Each one of you has distinct talents and gifts that can help others. Be open to the gifts I make available to you. Be willing to be a channel through which I can help others.

Avail yourself of Christian fellowship, and be open to the people I put in your path. I use many people to help you with your daily problems. I can even use the ones you consider your enemies.

Listen for My voice. In the quietness of your prayer time, listen for My voice. I am always ready to talk to you. The question is, are you ready to listen?

Know how pleased I am that you are in that place, in that time frame, in the flow of the anointing where miracles can be created, in your life and in the lives of all I send who come under your influence.

Love! Love! Love! Never be caught not loving. It is only as you live in love that you fulfill My will in your life. Let your life be inspired by love, controlled by love, and driven by love. Let love rule every area of your life.

My dear child, many are the seeds you have planted that have grown up in Me and are now full-grown trees—ready to bear much fruit. Take and eat of the fruit of the Spirit.

Take Joy and see your strength increase.

Take Peace and your love will be secure.

Take Patience and you will overcome every adverse situation in your life.

Take Gentleness and your conduct will always reflect My love.

Take Goodness and spread My love to all you meet.

Take Faith, for it is love's confidence.

Take Meekness, for it is love's humility.

Take Temperance, for it is love's victory.

Yes, take and eat of the fruit of the Spirit. Eat and live that your joy may be full as you continue to bear much fruit.

Remember, My child, you are excellent because My Spirit is in you. I love you. I love you with an everlasting love.

Love, God

I WILL HELP YOU

Dear One:

I have heard your cry! Your prayers have reached My ears! I will not fail you! I will show you My ways. I will teach you the right path to take.

I know that you are not a proud person. You do not flaunt your self-sufficiency by refusing to conform to the ways of proper Christian conduct that I have taught you in My Word.

Yes, I know, sometimes you go astray, but your heart is so tender towards Me and My ways that when I speak to you about it, you quickly yield yourself to pattern your life on the biblical standard that I have set before you.

I know that your reverence toward Me and My Word springs from real love. This love is so deep that you desire to shun anything and everything that could offend Me.

I know your heart is set on perfect obedience to Me and My Word. Because of this, you often berate yourself when you fall short of that perfection. I want to remind you that I look on the heart. I know your heart is set on Me, and I know that your desire is to perfectly obey Me in every facet of your life.

I love you, and because you have responded to My love, there is a bond that grows between us. You and I are good friends. Because of that, I want to spend some quality time in fellowship with you. I want us to talk together. Tell Me about the things that are bothering you. I want to know about your frustrations, too. Tell me how I can be of help in any other way. Just ask Me. I want to be able to promote happiness and prosperity in every area of your life.

Please don't forget to talk to Me about the things that bring you joy, too. Tell me in detail about the victories in your life. Think about them. Talk to me about them, for this will build up a confidence within you that will help keep the bad from overwhelming the good.

Hear me and don't forget these words—there is nothing in this world that you and I cannot overcome together. Mark My words well, and share them with other people. I want everyone to know, "I will help you!"

Love, God

YIELDING YOUR WILL

My Dear Child:

I have heard your prayer of frustration. I know you have so much to do that, at times, you're not sure how you'll get it all done.

Believe me, with My help, you are capable of doing any of these things. But you must continue to ask as you have been. Then most importantly, you must believe that your mountain of things can be accomplished through you by Me.

Always remember that it is My power that makes things happen. My power and your will. Before I can ever use My power within you, you have to be willing to allow Me. You must choose Me.

Very often My children forget about their free will. They groan and moan about their problems. They despair of My mercy. Yet, I have said since the very beginning of creation: humans have a free will. Is not a gift more precious and more appreciated when it is given freely? Does a gift bring you joy when you force someone to give it to you? Give some thought to this. You know the answer in your heart.

If man, who is imperfect, desires to be honored by gifts that are freely given, how much more must I, your Lord and your God, your Comforter, desire that you give freely to Me.

Some of My children ask themselves, "What can I give? I have nothing of value." Never think this of yourself! None of My creations are without value. What I desire more than anything is the gift of yourself.

I want you to glue yourself to Me—totally and completely—so that I can complete My work in you.

You were created in My image and likeness, but your preoccupation with material things has kept you from maturing and developing as much as you can.

Your free will has not always chosen Me. Therefore, I have been unable to mold you more completely into My image. Your free will stands in My way. When you learn to ask for My help; when you learn to rely on My help; when you learn to accept My help; when you learn how to help others, you will grow into the more perfect image I desire for you.

Pray! Praise My name! Fast! Love yourself! Then you will have a greater capacity to love others and Me.

Never forget that perfect love casts out fear. My love for you is perfect. Receive it.

Love, God

POWER OF PRAISE

Dear Child:

Make a joyful noise unto the Lord! Let your lips sing praises unto the God of your salvation. Enter into the blessings of Almighty God. Enter into His courts with praise. Rejoice! Rejoice! Rejoice in the Lord always, and again I say, Rejoice!

My dear child, if you only knew the power of praise. I have placed many of My teachers, pastors, and evangelists in your path to teach you the power of praise. You believe, yet you still do not fully realize that it is one of your mightiest weapons.

It is impossible to remain sad and depressed when you are singing praises to Me. You can praise yourself through any situation you find yourself in, and you can praise yourself into the blessings of God.

The thief has been trying to devour you, but he cannot. No, he cannot! He is defeated, and you have the authority to get him out of your family, out of your business, and out of your life completely. Satan has to flee when you are submitted to Me and resist him in the name of Jesus. He has no choice. It isn't maybe he'll go, maybe he'll stay. No, a thousand times, No! When you resist Satan in the name of Jesus, he has to flee.

What My children don't realize is that Satan lurks around using his tools of discouragement and deception to try to make a comeback. If you give in to those thoughts, if you worry and meditate on the thoughts Satan puts into your mind, you give him an open door to return.

Cast those imaginations down. Take every thought captive. Pull down Satan's stronghold and think only about things that are pure, that are true, that are lovely and of good report.

Clear your mind of negative thoughts. Concentrate on Me and My Word.

Confess with your mouth that I am the Lord God who has delivered you. It is My Son who was wounded for your transgressions. It was He who was bruised for your guilt and iniquities. It was He who was chastised so that you could obtain peace. It was He who bore the stripes on His back so that you could be healed and made whole.

These things are yours, My child. These things I have obtained for you. Enter into the life of deliverance and wholeness that is yours, and praise Me, Whose you are and Whom you serve!

Love, God

SEEK YOUR FATHER FIRST

My Child:

Where can you run, except to Me? You go here and there, to this one and that one. You seek answers. You try solutions, and in the end, you come to Me. When will you learn to begin with Me?

When you face a mountain, don't exhaust all human solutions and then finally turn to Me. Come to Me first! How I wish you'd give Me first consideration in all that you do! How I wish you'd consult Me first instead of last!

I am your God, your Father. I care for you, and I am ready to help you in every life situation that you encounter.

Are your burdens too heavy? Are your cares too numerous? Then cast them on Me. I will carry them for you.

Are you in a state of confusion as to what to do, when to do it, and how to do it? Then come to Me. Ask Me, and I will give you peace. Ask Me, and I will give you wisdom.

Are *things* causing you problems? Is your car not working? I can help you. I can lead you to people who know how to fix cars, boats, houses, etc.

Are *people* causing you concern? I can give you favor with people.

Are *you* your own problem? Are you talking too much about your circumstances and not looking to Me? Are you wavering to and fro? Are you accepting defeat by not even considering victory? Are you simply doing nothing and letting the winds of life toss you to and fro?

If you are under the circumstances instead of on top of them, if you're defeated instead of victorious, if you are depressed by things and people around you, if the light and life have gone out of your life, then you need to run back to the Source of light and life. You need to run to Me not *from* Me.

Why do you insist on doing things on your own? Why do you let Satan tell you that you are now mature enough to solve your own problems?

Why do you feel inadequate because you have to depend on Me? Do you think you will ever outgrow your need of Me? Do you think you'll ever get to the place where you can be self-sufficient? Believe me, you never will, for I am the Source of everything you need.

Just as you cannot possibly store a lifetime of food and provisions, you can never come to Me just once and never need to come back again.

You can never store enough provisions from Me to last forever! You must keep coming to Me for fresh spiritual food, fresh joy, and fresh daily strength, for that is how I created you.

Love, God

JOY OF INDEPENDENCE

My Child:

Apart from Me, you are nothing, and you can do nothing. You and I are a team. We work together. Therefore, we must fellowship with each other.

You need My direction in your life; but in order to receive it, you must come to Me to get it. I cannot minister to you if you hold Me off, if you do not come to Me. I cannot. I will not force you to do anything against your will, for I am a God of love.

Have you noticed, child, how it pleases you to do something for someone who asks for help? Those who trust you enough to ask you to do them a favor become your close friends. It pleases you to help others.

I have seen you offended when someone you love has a need and chooses to suffer instead of asking you to help them. When you realize later that they suffered needlessly when you had the power and the willingness to help them, you were offended. "Why didn't you ask me for help?" you question your friend.

I say to you, "Child, why don't you ask Me for help? I cannot give it unless you ask, for that is a principle—Ask and you shall receive."

Child, you will never be independent of Me. You may outgrow your dependence on your human parents, but you will never be independent of Me. For I am the Source of everything you need. As long as you seek Me, all things will be added to you.

Child, you are in control of your life. I do not automatically supply your every need. You must ask, and I will gladly give. You must call upon Me, and I am sure to answer. You must tell Me that you love Me, and you will be able to discern how much I love you.

Do not be deceived into thinking you have outgrown Me. You will never outgrow Me. It is rebellious to run from Me and think you are sufficient in yourself. Apart from Me, you can do nothing. The race you are running can be won if you run it with Me. I have called you. You are My own. I am with you, and I will never leave you. So, don't you willfully leave Me or wander away from Me!

Love, God

SALVATION

Oh, My Child:

How I delight in daily communing with you. How I desire for you to be able to see yourself the way I see you!

Before you were born, I knew you. I saw you complete, entire, wanting nothing. I infused you with everything you needed to be successful. I saw to it that you would meet people who could and would teach you and guide you into becoming My child. I saw to it that you heard the Word. I have set before you everything you need for success. And, child, you have responded well. I am pleased.

What joy there was in heaven when you made Jesus the Lord of your life! We rejoiced at that moment when you said, "Lord Jesus, I believe that You are the Son of God.

"I believe that You died and were raised from the dead. I ask You, Lord Jesus, to come into my heart. I repent of all of my sins. I lay all of my past at Your feet. I place all of my future in Your hands. Jesus, fill me with Your Holy Spirit. Heavenly Father, I am Your child. Thank You for saving me."

At that very moment, when you made Jesus Lord and asked Him to take charge of your life, you became a new creation. You became perfect inside.

Oh, yes, I know that you didn't immediately lose all of your old habits of the flesh. But, child, I want you to know that at the moment that you became My child, your spirit was recreated. Behold, old things passed away and all things were made new.

Now, child, the rest of your Christian walk simply involves bringing what's inside of you to the surface, and out into the world. It's letting your recreated spirit grow and mature and control your mind and your body so that when people will see you, they will see Me.

People will know that you are different, because now that you have been born again, I dwell in you and you dwell in Me. I am working in you and through you.

It delights My heart that you are now in My family. Heaven wouldn't be the same without you!

Love, God

GROWING UP SPIRITUALLY

Dear Child:

I am glad that you are single-minded in serving Me. It pleases Me too, that you are renewing your mind with the Word of God.

My dear, eye has not seen nor ear heard, neither has it entered into the heart of man what great things I have prepared for you. Much good awaits you. All that is necessary is for you to grow up in Me.

Just as a mother and father do not entrust responsibilities that are beyond the mental, physical, and emotional capabilities of their newborn babies—so I, your heavenly Father, do not require that you immediately do a work that is beyond you.

In the natural world, it takes years to mature. But in the spiritual world, you don't have to wait years and years to reach the point where you are capable of fulfilling the call that I have placed on your life.

No, child, there is no limit to how fast you can grow up spiritually, and there is no limit to how high you can grow spiritually. A born-again believer who sets his eye on Me, determines to be like Me and never looks back, can quickly surpass a person who simply has been plodding along for years.

This should not surprise you, for it is so even in the natural. Many people who are new to a job exceed the workmen who have been on the same job for years. Why? Simply because of their desire to serve, their desire to learn more, their desire to improve as much as they possibly can.

Child, don't ever be satisfied to stay on one spiritual level forever. You must continue to move forward. To remain static is to stagnate. There is no such thing as "arriving" spiritually. You should always be in the process of becoming better and better.

I try never to frustrate you by showing you all of your responsibilities and the jobs you are to accomplish in one sitting. That will only give you a feeling of hopelessness. No, I just unveil what I want you to do now at this moment of your life. When you achieve that, I show you something else that you are capable of doing if you are willing and obedient. That's the only prerequisite—to be willing and obedient.

Together we can do it. Together we will do it. We can co-labor in the vineyards to bring all men into the knowledge of the truth that Jesus is Lord! It is My desire to work with you, in you, and through you. My child, we need each other. The world needs the truth.

Love, God

ENCOURAGEMENT

Dear Child:

Be encouraged! Do not despair! I have not forgotten you. Yes, I know sometimes it seems like I have, but I have not! I know that sometimes you feel lost.

Sometimes you feel like you are working and studying and accomplishing nothing. That is a lie from the devil. I have a blueprint for your life, and you are in perfect alignment with that plan.

I know everything about you. I see what you are doing. I know your thoughts at every moment in time. Day by day I observe the good deeds that you do, and it is I who will give you eternal rewards for your faithfulness, for I am not unrighteous to forget your work and labor of love that you have done in My name.

I know exactly where you are, for you see, I am walking with you. I am ahead of you. I am beside you. I am behind you. I am always with you. My hand of blessing is on your head. You can never be lost, for I know where you are at all times.

I am all-knowing. My understanding is unlimited. I am all-powerful. My power is absolute. I am everywhere. I am present everywhere at the same time. Nothing is too hard for Me. You need to say daily, "Nothing is too hard for God; therefore, nothing is too hard for me because I am in Him and He is in me."

Remember, it is I who have called you into ministry. It is I who have prepared the way for you to learn of Me and My ways. It is I who have directed your steps, and I am still directing your steps. In My Word, I have promised you so many things. Claim those promises. Stand on them.

Don't for one moment entertain the lies of the devil. He would have you think that I am not faithful, but you have My promises and you have My oath that I will not change My mind about fulfilling those promises. You can count on these—My promises and My oath. I always do what I say I will do. It is impossible for Me to lie.

I say to you right now, "My child, I am well pleased with you. The love and kindness you show to others is evidence that you know Me and love Me. Thank you for being obedient to My Word. Continue to be diligent and in due season, you will reap."

Know that I am well pleased with you.

Love, God

DILIGENCE

My Child:

This is it! Now is the time to act! Don't get caught in the trap of "someday I will do something for God." When you consistently put off like that, nothing gets done.

This tendency to put off doing things is one of the great problems with humanity today. No one ever intends to procrastinate, but if you put off doing when you should be doing, somehow it is easier to put it off again and again. Eventually you forget about it, and it never gets done or someone has to do it for you.

A good thought unspoken cannot bless anyone. A letter unwritten cannot be read. A witty invention not produced cannot help people. A race not begun cannot be won.

Look around you! Who are the doers and movers in the world today? Are they the ones who sit around and wait until a job gets to be monumental before they decide to tackle it? Or are they the ones who do each little job as the need arises?

Who has the nicest lawn? Is it the man who lets the grass get a foot tall, then spends hours working at cutting? Or is it the person who spends an hour each week cutting an inch at a time? Whose house is consistently neat? Is it the person who does nothing all week, then hires a maid to clean it in one day? Or is it the person who daily cleans clutter and dusts as the need arises?

Tasks are accomplished in this world by people who work a little at a time—day in and day out.

This is also how you grow up physically. A baby is born. Years later, the child is full grown. It happened so gradually each day that you hardly even noticed when it happened. Learn from this. This is how one grows spiritually.

To grow up spiritually, read the Word of God daily. Hear the Word. Meditate on the Word. Confess the Word. Pray daily. Spend time with Jesus alone. Develop relationships with people who can help you grow spiritually.

Forsake not the assembling together with other believers in a local church body, for you have need one of another.

Regularly give of your tithes and offerings. "Give, and it shall be given unto you; good measure, pressed down, and shaken together, and running over, shall men give into your bosom" (Luke 6:38).

My child, as you do these things, you will become an active doer of the Word. Don't put it off! Do it now!

Love, God

FIGHT THE GOOD FIGHT OF FAITH

My Dear Parent:

"Call unto me, and I will answer thee, and shew thee great and mighty things, which thou knowest not" (Jeremiah 33:3).

Watch! Be alert and see the salvation of the Lord working in your life and through your family. I am in the business of creating successes. All I need is pliable material that will yield and obey My leading, for truly I direct the steps of My children. All that My children have to do is get in step with Me.

How do you get in step with Me? The starting point is through prayer. Divine connections are made when you seek Me in prayer and then obey Me.

Next, determine to let Me be in control. Let Me direct your life. Let Me be the Chairman of the Board. Let Me be at the controls of your life. It will be for your benefit, so you can be a blessing to others.

Don't hide your talents. Take off that bushel basket and give Me the firstfruit of your talents. Turn them over to Me! Then turn right around and use them for My glory and benefit. I am in need of all the gifts and talents I can recruit for My cause.

Also, as a contributing member of My family, I need you to be successful in all that you do!

You have done remarkably well these past years with your limited knowledge of Me and My Word. I have stepped in where you could not fulfill your part. I have protected your children and family from any mistakes you may have made.

Now that you have more knowledge, you know how to fight the enemy—the evil one. You are suited up in My armor for battle, and now you are fighting in the Spirit with the same vengeance you fight with to protect your loving family.

Get in step with Me by fighting the good fight of faith! All of My blessings and resources are yours. I am withholding nothing from you. "The kingdom of heaven suffereth violence, and the violent take it by force" (Matthew 11:12). Become violent for Me in the Spirit, and take what the devil is withholding from you.

All of My blessings are yours for the asking; for the taking. Receive them in Jesus' name! And then with a loud voice, gather your children around and praise, "Hallelujah!"

Love, God

THE INFINITE LOVE OF GOD

My Dear Child:

My love for you reaches above the highest, below the lowest, and beyond measure in all directions. It reaches infinitely beyond where your natural love ends. My love and mercy reach into the nether reaches of darkness, error, and sin to attain the object of My love—you.

My love for you is revealed in that I redeemed you from sin. This divine love looked past all the iniquity and wickedness that Jesus on the cross became for you. I saw what you, My children, could be because of Him. My love overpowered all the darkness and sin to obtain you, whom I have loved since before the beginning of time.

I long to reveal to you the breadth, length, depth, and width of my love! I have loved you with an everlasting kind of love. Therefore, with divine loving-kindness I have I drawn you to Me.

It is you, precious one, that I long to bring into My family, right now at this very moment. It is so easy to be in My family. Just turn to Me with a contrite heart and confess: "Oh God, because I am a sinner, I come to you in Jesus' name. I'm sorry for my sins. I ask You, Lord, to forgive me, come into my heart, and make me Your child."

In My family, you will learn not to be concerned with being popular. This will profit you nothing. Do you not know that being the world's friend is being God's enemy? (James 4:4) Therefore, if you choose to be a friend of the world, you are taking your stand as an enemy against Me.

Lift yourself up! Lift your soul and body up! Lift them to the level of your spirit. All three of My natures walk among the high places. The Son does not lag behind and live in squalor. The Holy Spirit does not rebel against Me. So also must you be like Me. You are a triune being, and as such, each of your natures, body, soul, and spirit, are to live on things from above. You are to walk in high places.

Write My infinite words of love on your heart. Carry them around your neck. Meditate on them day and night, and you shall walk in high places and be prosperous and have good success. That is because I love you with an infinite love.

Love, God

MINISTRY Of GIVING

Dear One:

You are a family of givers. When you give into the ministry of our Lord Jesus Christ, then the gospel can go forth in power and strength. No longer give your money into a "Dead Sea."

No longer support men and women who do not hold out the Word of God. Let your criteria for giving be, "Does that ministry preach the Word?" The Word will save the world. Either you proclaim My Word or you must help others proclaim it by your giving.

When you give to the cause of My gospel, I shall bless you— not just a hundredfold, but unlimitedly.

I gave My all. I gave 100 percent in that I gave My only Son to die for you and yours, just as a seed must die before it can bring forth a harvest.

A harvest came on Pentecost when 120 believers gathered and were added to My Kingdom followed by 3,000 more who were added as a result of the 120, and more added daily. You can help add to the Kingdom by your giving. I am not only talking of giving financially, I am talking of giving your time, your talent, your prayers, and your love. Most of all your love.

I have a stockpile of blessings for you! They are yours! You claim them when You call your harvest in. Have I not said that the harvest is ripe, but there are not many who are willing to go out in the fields and bring it in? Have I not said that? Bring in the harvest, child. Bring it in!

The world is crying for Me, and you have the answer— Jesus! Don't withhold Him from them. They cry. They seek. They stumble. They are in the dark. You have the light. Let your light shine, and I shall shatter their darkness.

You will not have to seek them. I will put people in your path, so all you have to do is be a witness for Me. Show the world who I am by how you live. Show the sick and the dying how I redeemed you, and they will seek that redemption.

Lead them to Me, and I will do the rest. All I need is a willing vessel to show how My Word can transform a person who will boldly give Me the glory for every good thing in his life. All I need is a willing vessel who will plant the seed.

Bring the firstfruits of your time, your love, and your finances into My storehouse and see if I will not open up the windows of heaven and pour out a blessing on you.

Love, God

GOD'S PROSPERITY

My Dear Child:

And what is it you need today? Do you need peace? Jesus is the Prince of Peace.

Do you need finances? I am your Provider. Do you need a friend? I am your Friend who sticks closer than a brother.

Do you need healing? By Jesus' stripes you were healed.

What do you need? Is it that you feel so lost and alone that you cannot even isolate what it is that you need to feel safe, secure, joyful, and fulfilled? If that is the position you are in right now, then turn aside from every weight that besets you. Cast your care on Me, and begin to rejoice in Me! Praise Me and worship Me!

Begin right now to thank Me for every good thing that has ever happened in your life. Thank Me for what I am doing now. Thank Me for the good things you are believing for. Yes, thank Me for them, for if you ask Me for anything in Jesus' name, I will give it to you. You already have it in the spiritual realm. Just thank Me. Release your faith. Keep your eyes on Me.

Faith is the bridge that connects heaven to earth. How I want you to prosper and be in health! Everything you need was bought for you at the cross. Yes, I paid the price for you. You are redeemed. Have you forgotten all that is yours? You must remember your inheritance, and you must claim your inheritance. I can do nothing for you that I have not already done.

My child, you need to enter into My promises. All you have to do is first seek the Kingdom of God. Here you will learn what is yours, and then you release My power to operate in your life. Seeking the Kingdom stills the enemy, for he cannot gain a foothold in a mind that is stayed on Me.

Yes, My child, I will that you prosper and be in health, even as your soul prospers. You cannot have one without the other. Your mind, will, and emotions must operate in peace.

My precious one, I sprinkle My Son's blood over you with living faith in His name. Peace is flooding your spirit, your soul, and your body. Peace is yours. Peace. Be still and know that I am God. Peace.

Close your eyes now, and let My peace flood your soul and let Me take care of you.

Love, God

ENCOURAGEMENT FOR TEACHERS

My Dear Teacher:

Believe in Me and trust Me, for in all that happens I have a purpose. Continue to pray and cast all your cares on Me. Do not try to carry them alone. I care for you!

Continue to desire the unity of the Spirit that you have so longed for, because I will grant you the desires of your heart. I wish that there would be no schism in the body, but that the members would have the same care one for another. I know your wish is the same. Remember, your treasure is not on earth where it's computable, but your reward is in heaven!

Blessed are you who mourn for My children. You will be comforted by the Holy Spirit. Blessed are you because your meekness has enabled you to bring about the rare quality of communication on the same level of the students you teach.

You shall inherit the earth. Blessed are you because you hunger and thirst after righteousness. Blessed are you because you are merciful to those I have placed in your care. I will have unlimited mercy on you. I will bless you because of your pure heart. Because you are a peacemaker and you win battles in the wars of this world, you will be blessed.

You are a light in this world, and your light cannot be hidden. Your light is set upon a hill for all to see. Therefore, let your light continue to shine before little children. You are My witness that your students and their families may see your good works.

Give the glory to Me, and I will not only reward your deeds on earth, but I will also bless others through you.

My dear teaching servant, when preparations for class have been readied, then take no thought for tomorrow. Seek the

117

Kingdom of righteousness. Rejoice in Me, and leave your problems in My hands. I provide for you day by day.

You are not confounded. You are not perplexed. Your life is not thrown into disorder as long as you anchor yourself in Me. I have given you all things that pertain to life and godliness.

Care for your responsibilities as they come, but don't take thought of it. I don't want you to be concerned about anything. When you are able to release worrying, when you are able to lean on Me and trust Me, you will begin to live the victorious life. You will be free to do what is right and necessary in your life, as you care for My children.

Love, God.

OVEREATING

Dear One:

How it grieves My Spirit to see the physical condition you are in right now. I did not create you to glorify Satan in your body. No! I created you in My image. I created you to glorify Me.

No, I am not ashamed of you. No, I don't love you less. Because you see, I don't see you as you look physically. I see you as I created you to be.

I see you healed, healthy, whole, vitally alive, and able to move with the freedom and agility of a young child. This is what I have for you. Yet you allow yourself to be tempted. You have yielded to every thought of temptation from Satan. You, like Adam, have failed the test of food. But you have the power to resist.

Within you is My Word. Within you is My Spirit. Within you is all that you need in order to resist and defeat Satan in the realm of your thought life, for that's where you are defeated. Your failure isn't in overeating. No, your failure is in meditating on food. You become fat in your mind long before your body manifests the results of overeating.

"Why do I overeat?" you cry in anguish inside your mind and your spirit. Each time you eat when and what you know you're not supposed to eat, you condemn yourself, and right there and then you determine in your heart never to succumb to food again! But then you do again—and again. Satan has you on a merry-go-round, and you think you can't get off. But you can, and it's so simple!

Start by humbling yourself before Me. Present your body to Me a holy, living sacrifice. Determine to make your body the best you can make it for Me to dwell in, because that's where I dwell on earth. You are the temple of the Holy Spirit. Yes, you and your brothers and sisters.

How much would you scurry about to clean your house if the president were coming to visit? Well, My child, I am not coming to visit. I am already here, living inside of you. Meditate on that daily.

See Me in you, living and moving and performing My work here on earth through you.

See Me living in you daily. Keep that thought uppermost in your mind, and then you shall have victory over food. Then you shall be able to resist, for just as you would not throw mud on the floor of your clean house before company comes, you will not throw unhealthy food in an unhealthy amount into your temple, because that would defile My temple here on earth.

Love, God

SHARE THE NEED FOR DISCIPLINE

My Dear child:

It grieves Me to see you hurt. You think you are unworthy because you have not conquered food, but you are worthy. Yes, you are! You are My child, and I am well pleased with you. I know the desires of your heart, because I put them there.

Bring the desires of your heart into manifestation in your life by praying in the Spirit. It is through intercession that you will obtain the victory. Whenever any thought of food comes into your mind, it is time for you to begin interceding in the Spirit.

Be aware that I am living within you. I live in your temple. Just as you keep your mind pure by thinking of Me, keep your body as it should be, by recognizing My presence, and by practicing stewardship in your eating. You will be victorious. The battle is Mine. The victory can be yours. Go forth in confidence and power and might. Let the "you" I have created within shine through for all the world to see.

Soon, very soon, your body will follow the guidelines set up by your spirit, and you shall be the witness for Me that you have always desired to be—not only in your spirit and your mind, but also in your body. Your victory will be an encouragement to many, and it will add long years to your life.

Soon you will have more time to serve Me, because you have disciplined your body to eat right. Shout Hallelujah! I rejoice over the victory you can receive this day.

What is holding you back from this victory? Why are you always so willing to pray for others, but you are not willing to accept the prayers of others on your behalf? Why aren't you free to receive and accept gifts? Tell Me, child; tell Me now, not because

I need to know what is holding you back, but because you need to confess what is holding you back.

Child, to achieve physical victory in overindulging, command fear and embarrassment to leave in Jesus' name. Get rid of the fear of exposing your needs and weakness to others. You must risk being vulnerable. You must risk sharing yourself with others. In this way you are not fighting this fight alone. The prayers of righteous intercessors will avail much.

Love, God

SAFE FROM THE WORLD

Dear Child:

Confusion, sin, and chaos were all around Noah. Yet he remained apart from it. He isolated his spirit and was not led astray.

I gave the people of Noah's day an opportunity to turn from their wicked ways, but they would not do so. The sin on the earth had polluted almost everything. Only Noah and his family were obeying Me. So I sent the flood to rid the earth of sin. Before I sent the flood, I gave Noah clear instructions of what to do to save his family. Noah obeyed!

For 120 years Noah worked on the ark that would keep him and his family and all the animals safe from the flood. He did not keep this operation a secret. During all the construction time Noah's neighbors saw the huge vessel going up in his backyard. Besides this, Noah daily warned his neighbors about the impending flood. People had time to repent and be saved, but they chose not to believe. They went on living their lives, with a future of doom looming over them. They could have chosen life instead of death, and then they too would have been saved by entering into the safety of the ark.

Finally the floods came and ended the earth's sin and corruption, but Noah, his family, and the animals were saved in the ark because they were obedient.

Today there is as much sin and corruption in the world, but no matter how corrupt it gets, I will not destroy the earth by flood waters again, because I promised Noah that I would not. I have sent another ark to save My people. This ark is My only Son Jesus. He is an ark of safety whose door is open wide to whosoever will come unto Him.

Those who seek salvation may enter into this ark by the new birth—by accepting Jesus as their Lord and Savior. This will allow them to remain warm and secure in the ark, protected from the sin and corruption of the world. Security in the ark is remaining in Christ.

Abiding in Christ guarantees that no matter how the winds of confusion, sin, and chaos rage about you, you shall be safe! Enter in, I welcome you.

Love, God

POWER OF YOUR WORD

My Child!

Death and life are in the power of the tongue! Whatever your present circumstances are now, they have been created by the words you have spoken in the past. Words are containers. They contain creative force.

I spoke the world into existence with words. The earth was void and without form (Genesis 1:2), and I said, "Let there be light," and there was light! I said, "Let there be a firmament in the midst of the waters," and it was so! Words are a creative force. Just as I create with My words, so do you create with your words.

The world recognizes the power of words. When a person is buying a car, the salesman's primary purpose is for you to say, "Yes, I'll buy the car." At the sound of the word "yes," all of the action necessary to process the sale of the car goes into effect. The word "no" would not have caused that same response.

With your words you choose your companions, you choose what you'll eat in a restaurant, you choose the house you'll buy, you choose the job you'll have, and you choose the person you'll marry.

There is always a choice. You can say, "Yes" or "No." You say "I do" and the person who stands beside you becomes your lifetime partner. To remain silent would be saying "No."

You even choose your God by the words you speak. If you confess Jesus as your Lord and Savior, then I am your God. If you reject Me either by saying "No" or just by remaining silent, you've chosen Satan as your god.

Meditate on your life right now. Is someone angry with you? Are you angry with someone? Can you trace back what caused the anger? It was words, wasn't it? Someone said something and you responded and then they responded—and the cycle began.

Think of the times you've been hurt. What was the cause of the hurt? You are hurt either because someone said something hurtful to you or because they neglected to say something nice to you.

Words. Words have power! You make people happy or you make people sad by the words you speak to them. The person who can control his or her tongue proves that he has control over himself.

Submit your tongue to the control of My Holy Spirit. Fill yourself daily with My Word, and watch your very own tongue blossom with life!

Love, God

I LOVE TO BE YOUR EVERYTHING

My Dear Child:

I want you to love Me and My children, and I want you to love yourself, because you are a fruitful branch.

I want to use you. You have made yourself available. Soon, very soon, My ability will become more and more a part of You because you shall turn more and more to Me in My Word. And what you hear and see and study shall be yours to help make you an able minister of the gospel.

What you learn shall help set others free. All you have to do is study and expect to learn, to understand, to retain—and teach in a way that will impart knowledge to others in a supernatural way.

I have called you to be a teacher of many, but first I must teach you.

Turn to Me before studying, and I will multiply your time so that you will not have to go over the material over and over in order to learn it. Yes, I will multiply your time for I have more things for you do so, and there is no more time to give you.

You do hear Me. You do know what I want you to do and in the order I want it done.

Seek Me first. That's the only priority you need to know right now. And confess daily that you are led by My Spirit, and each day you will do what I want you to do, for I will send the ones to you right now who need help, and I will minister to them through you.

I long to have a family, and I long to have a personal relationship with each member of that family. I long to be all that everyone needs, for I have the solutions each one needs.

I long for more people to go into the harvest field and gather My children in. I long to have all My children know who I am and what I am capable of and how much I want to help them live the victorious life.

I long to see My children fight their own battles with the weapons and war strategy I have given them.

I delight to see My children take back from Satan all that he has stolen from them. I long to see them grow up to full maturity, being able to fight their own battles, being free to come to Me when they need help.

Love, God

DIRECTION

My Dear:

If you can believe, all things are possible to them who believe. My child, you must believe in your heart that something is possible to achieve before you can receive it.

You have to set a standard for what you want to be. You have to know what you want to achieve in life in order to know what goals to set and what direction to take. No one arrives at a desired destination by merely wandering around aimlessly.

Where are you going? What are you planning to be? What are your goals in life? What have you achieved so far? Are you well on your way to becoming what you want to be? Do you really know what you want to be?

Do not be discouraged, My child! I have a plan for your life, and I can create within you the right desires for your life. You can have My will and My purpose for your life. What is My will for you? It is My Word! If you want to know My will, read My Word. You can find My plan, My direction for your life in My Word.

Dear one, I want to show you My ways. I want to teach you My paths. I want to lead you in My truth. I want to teach you all things that pertain to life and godliness, and I do all these things through My Word. You can find My plan, My direction for your life in My Word.

My Word is light. My Word is life. My Word is health and prosperity. My Word is a lamp unto your feet. My Word is all you need to go from where you are to where I want you to be.

In My plan is life forevermore with an abundance of daily peace and blessings.

Step aside with Me. Find a quiet spot to tune into Me. Search your heart to make sure your motives measure up to My standard. Establish your heart to believe and receive My goals for you!

Love, God

CHOOSE LIFE WITH YOUR WORDS

My Precious Child:

I am always watching over you. I am continually making intercession on your behalf. The angels hearken to My Words, and they are working to bring them to pass in your life. Speak My Words, and you yourself commission the angels.

My Words bring life. My Words bring light. My Words bring love. My Words bring peace. My Words bring prosperity. My Words bring joy. My Words bring health. My Words bring every good thing that you need and want in this life and in the life to come. My Words do not return to Me void. They will never pass away.

Your mouth is a storehouse of words, and you hold the key to it. You don't have to speak every word that comes into your mind, for some that come into your mind are not from Me.

I want you to remember that your words are coins in the Kingdom of Faith. What will you buy today with the words of your mouth? Will it be life or death? The choice is yours.

Always remember that I love you! There may be troubles in your life, but when you look to Me, you won't see them because you will have your affections set on things above and not on things of this earth. I know that you love Me. You please Me very much because your heart is fixed on Me.

Because of My love, I hasten to remind you, do not be discouraged! Don't look at all that you have to do and wonder how you will ever be able to do it! Houses are not built in a day. Babies do not grow up in a year. Wars are not won in an instant. Things take time!

Just look how far you've come spiritually and physically. You've come a long way towards becoming the mature person that I have called you to be, and you will come much further mentally if you cast your cares on Me.

Just do the very best you can in everything you are called to do, and I will honor your best efforts in ways that will astound you and bring glory to Me and My Word.

What you must focus on now is what I called you to do. You be the best you can be at every stage of your development. Keep your eyes on Me and My Word, and I will do the rest.

Love, God

DELIVERANCE

My Dear Child:

Arise! Arise and shine, for I have delivered you! And at this moment I am here with you. Yes, I am! I'm by your side, waiting for you to turn to Me. Waiting for you to allow Me to help you.

Let go! Let go of the burdens that you're carrying. Let go of the cares you have taken upon yourself. Just let go. Give them to Me. Give them all to Me. Give them to Me one by one. Release those cares. Feel yourself lifted higher and higher as you give Me everything that has been weighing you down. Let go of everything that has you bound and depressed and discouraged. Those things are not from Me. In My Son's name, let go of everything that is oppressing you right now. Just let go! Let go!

That's right! Do it and be free in My Son's name. Be free to be what I've called you to be. My child, take a deep breath; hold it for a count of four. Now let out. Slowly exhale and as you do, the tension in your body will be washed away.

Again, My child, breathe in deeply. Breathe in the Holy Spirit. Inhale love; exhale love. Allow the Holy Spirit to do a mighty work within you. Allow the Holy Spirit to cleanse you, refresh you. Just meditate on His indwelling you and filling you with peace and contentment.

Again, breathe in the Holy Spirit and exhale love. You are exhaling love, because My love is in you. Love surrounds you. You are bathed in love, both within and without.

As you breathe in deeply, think of yourself as getting bigger and stronger inside as you allow the Holy Spirit to have full reign in you. As you exhale slowly, receive My love flowing through you to your surroundings. Now your presence has created peace in your own environment, because I am with you.

Love is there with you, in you, around you. People are affected by your presence because you walk in love.

Do not allow yourself to be bowed down with the spirit of heaviness. Instead, put on the garment of praise. Lift up those hands that hang down. Lift up your voice to God. Pray in the Spirit. Pray in the understanding, and magnify the Lord.

Now close your eyes and continue to praise My holy name, for I inhabit the praises of My people. Shout Hallelujah! You're free because I have set you free.

Love, God

LOVE IS YOUR GUIDE

Dear One:

My child, I am the healing light that shall flood your inner being and illuminate each and every little thing and each and every big thing that keeps you from loving yourself and Me completely.

Love is the most important thing that you must learn. Love is light. Love is life. It heals all wounds. It loosens all bonds. It illuminates all darkness. Love lights the way to truth, joy, and happiness.

Yes, love is the answer. It is the greatest gift I can give you. Love is what your spirit has been denied. I, your heavenly Father, will fill the void in you with My all-powerful love.

My Son, Jesus, will fill you with His all-healing love. The Holy Spirit will dwell in you and fill you with His all-knowing love. Your heart will ever be filled with My love because you have come to Me and chosen to be My child.

Come, child, come and fellowship with Me in love. I long to spend some time with you so that you can know Me as I know you. My child, if you know all that I am able and willing to do for you, you would never become discouraged in any situation.

You see, I know all about you. I know your fears. I know your desires, your strengths, and your weaknesses. I know your thoughts at every moment in time! There is nothing you can hide from Me, for I am all-knowing, I am all-powerful. I am present everywhere at the same time.

I can see where you are going. I know where you are. You cannot hide from Me. I walk ahead of you as your Shepherd. I walk behind you as your Rear Guard. I walk beside you as your Friend. I hold you in the palm of My hand.

I am with you always. My hand of blessing is on your head. You can never be lost for I know where you are at all times.

I am not telling you this to frighten you. I am telling you this to encourage you and make you feel secure. I want you to know who I am and what I am. I want you to know what I am able to do, but most of all, I want you to know what I am willing to do for you.

I am willing to use all of My power on your behalf. All that I am and all that I have are available to you because you are My child and I love you.

Love, God

GOD'S PROMISE

Dearest Child:

I perform My Word in your life because you believe it, confess it, and walk in love—and because I love you.

For this day, you must know and see in your spirit that you are truly seated with Me in heavenly places. You are far above the earthly realm, and you shall not move below again.

You will soar in a new way. You are free in a new way. In a new way, let Me undertake to more than abundantly meet every one of your needs.

As you have read My Word, as you have obeyed Me, as you have stood, I have lifted you to a new position. Therefore, I do what I promised to do, because today is a new day and the old shall not return.

I implore you to stay close to Me. Your battles are My battles. Obey Me explicitly, even when you think, humanly speaking, you should not. Stand and watch Me do a new work. Watch Me perform superabundantly above whatever you can think or imagine.

I look on the heart, and I see that your heart is fixed on Me.

Remember that I will never leave you nor forsake you. Just trust Me. All is well. Let My love flow through you. Yes, all is well. Walk in peace, the peace that I have given you that is beyond understanding. Never cease praising Me, for I inhabit your praises.

Because I am true to My Word, and you are true to Me in your praise, I am leading you in a new direction, a new opening up into a ministry you have not allowed yourself to envision.

High is the road I've called you to travel, and child, it will not be hard. It will not take long. It is ready to come forth, for you have been pregnant with the ideas and seeds for a long, long time.

The time is now at hand. Your foundation is strong. Your tree is well developed. The buds have blossomed. The fruit has developed, and now the harvest is here. Don't allow your fruit to rot on your tree.

As you produce, give. Give to others. Give to the world. Give and much more will be given to you.

Be what I've called you to be. Be a planter of seeds. Be a waterier of seedlings. Be a cultivator of trees. Be a producer of fruit.

Love, God

TAKING ON MY ATTRIBUTES

My Dear Child!

How many times you've begun! How many times you've set your course and started out in the direction I have called you, and you still seem not aware of what I have called you to do.

How much time and energy you spend trying to change your weaknesses, trying to discover them and turn them into strengths. That is admirable.

But, child, spend some time concentrating on your strengths, for they are many.

Come to Me in faith and humility and offer Me your strengths. Make your strengths available to Me. Allow Me to flow through you. Spend time alone with Me. The more you do so, the more you will take on My attributes.

A sword that remains in a hot fire does not become fire. But the sword takes on the attributes of the fire. It becomes hot, just as the fire is hot.

When you spend time alone with Me in close fellowship, you take on My attributes. When a child is adopted into a family, he gains the privileges of being an heir of his parents.

When you become a part of My family, by your own free will you become My child and an heir of salvation. An adopted child becomes an heir, but does not change and begin to look like his adopted parents immediately.

My children are different. Not only do you, as My adopted child, become an heir, but the more you fellowship with Me, the more you become like Me. So come apart and commune with Me early in your day, child. As you take on My attributes, you will do the work of the ministry with the same power and effectiveness that followed Me.

I love you, dear one.

Remember, all love comes from Me. The love you experience now is the perfect love that has always been available to you. It is in each one of My children. The reason you've found it now is because you've sought it. You've expected it. You've shown it to others, and this has unlocked it in them. They will know you are a Christian by your love.

The love you have for each other will give the loudest testimony any of you could ever speak. The greatest orator in the world could not convey My message of love to others as well as your expression of love for each other can bring others to Me.

I am the way. Follow Me.

Love, God

FULFFILL YOUR ROLE IN THE BODY OF CHRIST

My Beloved Child!

I shall not want! I shall not want! I shall not want for children in the Kingdom of God. Child, I shall not want, because the Body of Christ is coming together in a new way to do the work of ministry. Yes, My Body is coming together in a new way. I have called the Body together, and each part is responding just as you are responding.

You shall fulfill your part. No one else will have to do what I've called you to do because you have stepped forward to answer My call. You have answered the call to be a vital part of Christ's body, and you have put your hand to the plow. You have not turned back. Satan has tempted you to turn to the right and to the left, but you have steadfastly resisted. You have resisted Satan because you have submitted to Me. "Submit yourselves therefore to God. Resist the devil, and he will flee from you" (James 4:7).

How I long to hold you close to Me! How I yearn to fellowship with you daily! Come to Me, My child. Come to Me with all your burdens, and lay them at My feet. Release them. Let go of the cares. Just let go right now. Let go and let Me be your everything!

Let Me come into your life with a new freshness, a new anointing. A new joy and peace will sustain you through whatever trial you're facing. Yes, not only sustain you, but lift you up above the storms of life.

As long as you are in the world, storms will come into your life, but you are not to be tossed to and fro by the storms. There is no storm that can overcome you when you remember to call on Me. Use My name and use My Word.

Wait upon Me, and you shall mount up on wings like an eagle. You shall soar up in the heavens above the storms, and you shall not be touched by them. You shall look down and view the storms of life and see that they are insignificant when seen from My vantage point.

Stay close to My side. Stay above the storms of life, and you will not be tossed to and fro. You shall not be hurt. You shall not be harmed in any way, for you were made to be more than a conqueror. You have already won. I have fought the battle for you. I have defeated Satan for you.

Victory is yours in Jesus' name.

Love, God

MINISTERING TO OTHERS

My Dear Child!

You are a haven of rest. I did not tell you that I would encase you in a cocoon merely to protect you. No indeed! I have encased you in a cocoon so that you could invite others in with you.

You see, My child, the cocoon you are in is not skin tight. It is large, and it has the ability to expand to take others in. There are many chambers in that cocoon of yours where people can come and rest to be refreshed.

Yes, I have called you to be a haven of rest in a troubled world. I have called you to be a solid ship on a stormy sea. I have called you to be a harbor for people to be refreshed, refueled, and revitalized with natural rest, peace of mind, and godly peace.

They will come. I am sending them to you. Take them in, and allow them to draw from you whatever they need from Me. I am a faith God. If you are faithful in doing that for My children, I will see to it that you are never without resources to help others.

Yes, you shall live in the thousand fold return realm. Whatever you do to refresh your own mind, soul, and body, I will cause you to reap a hundredfold return. But first, you understand, My child, that you must do something; give Me something to multiply.

By grace I have already been feeding your spirit person supernaturally. You have recognized that a long time ago. Now it is time for you to seek Me even more so in My Word. Do it.

Prove Me now in this, My child. Spend some time in My Word. Spend some quiet time with Me daily, and I will be your haven of rest.

See yourself as a harbor of rest where people pull in daily—some for an hour, some for a day, some for just a few minutes of exhortation. But not only will you be that haven of rest in your natural surroundings, you will be able to bring that haven of rest to others in other locations.

I tell you now this day that I will never leave you nor forsake you. I am with you. I always was and always will be with you. Where you go, I go. Be attentive to My voice. You know My voice. I will tell you who needs ministry. As you minister, you will benefit as much if not more than they. This is inner healing.

Love, God

WAITING ON THE LORD

Dear Child:

"They that wait upon the Lord shall renew their strength; they shall mount up with wings as eagles; they shall run, and not be weary; and they shall walk, and not faint" (Isaiah 40:31).

Wait upon the Lord! My Son is the Lord of your life. Make Him Lord over your mind, and your body as you have made Him Lord of your spirit.

In everything you do, do it as to the Lord. Wait upon My Son, and He will renew your strength. You shall soar above all the storms of life with wings just as eagles. You shall labor for Me, but you shall not be weary. You shall not faint, for you have the mind of Christ, and you can do all things through Him. He is your strength. He is your joy. He is your Brother. He is My Son, and you are My child. You share equally with Him in My sight.

The love I have for you is the same as the love I have for Him. The faith I've given you is the same measure of faith I used to raise Him from the dead. Use your faith. Plant it as a seed. Plant it as a seed to help others. That seed will soon come to life, sprout, and then bloom for the harvest of a soul.

Pray for others without ceasing and you will be deeply affected, healed, and made more Christ-like. You will be prosperous in your soul and in your life. For My Word says, "Pray ye one for another that ye may be healed." Know that I watch over My Word to see that it is performed. And My Word will not return to me void but will accomplish that which it was sent out to accomplish (Isaiah 55:11).

I will reveal more and more of My Word to you. But it isn't revealed for you to just expound it and tell others. You must first digest it and make it a part of you. Digest My Word! Walk in the light of what I have revealed to you. When you do that, I will reveal more to you. Day by day you will grow in grace if you do this.

My child, seek ye first the Kingdom of God and all things you need will be given unto you.

Love, God

INTERCESSION

My Dear Child:

If you will get up early and go to work for Me as an inter-cessor, with the same diligence you get up and go to work to earn a living, I will pay you and make you richer than you ever could be in your day job.

Intercession in the greatest job-calling of all. In the interces-sory field there are vacancies; there are promotions; and there are rewards.

Child, there is such a need for intercessors. Daily I search for someone to stand in the gap and pray for some of My children who are in need, and I can find none. I look to send intercessors to the front lines in order to protect you from the fiery darts of the enemy, for you see, I do not wait until you are attacked to launch an offense to protect you. No, I don't. I call on intercessors to pray for you and others before the attack even begins. If I did not do that, you would be attacked more than you are.

Many a day, many an hour, many a moment has been preserved for you by the diligence of intercessors. It is time that you stand in the gap for others. It is time that you consistently pray, that you do it with the same diligence, the same determination, the same tenacity that you report to work on your job every day.

Oh yes, I know. Most everyone is diligent in getting up early, dressing, and going to work every day. Why? Because they are committed to give an honest day's work for an honest day's pay. But too few are willing to get up and pray; to intercede for even an hour a day. Yet, the rewards of doing so are so much greater than any job you could ever have.

Pray, pray, pray! Never stop praying! Be vigilant! Do not get so caught up in newspapers and conversations and television and entertainment. Be single-minded. Live each moment of your life as if I am right by your side watching you and cheering you on, because I am.

Why don't you now rush to the defense of those who are in our family, the family of God, with the same eagerness you pray for your personal family? It is only because you are not aware of the need.

I know that you would pray and pray and pray some more if you really understood the need and if you really grasped the importance of intercession. Make it your priority in life. Let it be the first thing you do in the morning and the last thing you do at night.

Please, My child, take the job of intercession seriously.

Love, God

TAKE AUTHORITY WITH CHRIST IN YOU

My Child:

Do not wonder any more if you are in My perfect will. Do not wonder if you are doing what I want you to do. Do not wonder why you do not have this or that. Do not wonder, for wondering is wavering and a mind that wavers is double-minded.

My Word says a double-minded man receives nothing from the Lord. Your eye must be single. Your faith fixed. For you cannot reach out and receive My blessings, you cannot receive My promises if you do not reach out. My blessings are always there. My promises are true.

Don't ever remain in the pit. It is no shame to be down every now and then, but it is an abomination to me for you to remain there. My hand is always there within a few inches to reach for you and grasp you and pull you out.

Now you know what stuff you're made of. Good fruit does not come from a bad tree. You have been grafted into the Vine. You have been grafted into the living Vine, and it is no longer you who live, but Christ lives in you. The life that you now live in the flesh is lived by the faith of the Son of God who loved you and gave Himself for you.

Satan took his best shot at you, and he could not destroy you. Yet you were letting small, insignificant things in comparison weigh you down and defeat you.

You have authority in this world. You have the authority of a believer. Use it to bind the so-called "strongman," who is Satan.

If a thief entered your home to rob you, you'd get a broom and chase him out physically if you had to. Why then don't you immediately use your broom, which is My Word, to chase out the evil one when he enters your home in such devious ways as in self-pity, depression, strife, discouragement, etc.?

The moment he enters and puts one small thing from his world into your home—that's the time to immediately chase him out. Don't let the devil run over your household! You are responsible for your household, because you've been given the name of Jesus to protect it.

Love, God

PROTECTION AND SECURITY

Dear One:

If ever you put spiritual laws and physical laws into motion that are detrimental to your well-being, I, in My mercy and grace, will reach down and make things right for you. It is not My perfect will that you suffer.

If you happen to wander out from under My umbrella of covering that protects you from the curses Satan has an opportunity to get a shot at you.

You know I cannot violate My Word. I do not violate My Word, even to Satan.

Therefore, even though I cannot step in and stop something because I do not have the legal right to, I do keep My Word. And My Word says, "My grace is sufficient for thee." There is no tribulation that you can ever find yourself in that I will not give you the necessary grace to withstand.

You are My general, leading a mighty army of believers to Me. When I need you most, you never falter. When the pressure is on, you behave right, because that's what's in your heart!

Out of the abundance of the heart the mouth speaks. And you speak words of life, not words of death. You speak words of faith, not fear. You speak faith filled words, because that's what's in your heart.

The Christ in you never falters. Now I command your body to come in line with My Word, "Body, be whole."

My promise: I, who have begun a good work in you, will see it to completion. You were created in My image. That means you have My spirit within. That means greater things than I do, will you do. This is the foundation of your faith.

Again I say, hold close to Me. Keep your eyes single and on Me. Be God-minded. Remember, you have not chosen Me, but I have chosen you that you should go and bring forth fruit; and that your fruit should remain. Whatever you ask in My name, I will give it to you.

So, My child, I say this to you, whatever you desire when you pray, believe that you receive it, and you will.

Yes, My dear, you may and shall take authority!

Love, God

VISTORY OVER SATAN'S SCHEMES

My Precious Child!

Stand tall, precious one. Stand tall. The fiery darts have been flung your way, but stand tall. They cannot penetrate. They cannot gain any ground and soon will turn another way, for they can't make any gain upon you, child.

Stand tall and know that you have heard My voice. I've seen your tears. I've heard your every prayer, and many good surprises are coming your way, one by one.

Know that I am the I Am. There is nothing lacking with Me, whether it be in provision, in wisdom, in knowledge, or in confidence. I lack nothing. And I desire My children to lack nothing. I desire you to lack nothing, so reach to Me for your everything, and I won't deny you.

Look to Me, child, and I will continue to teach you new things. I will continue to teach you all things. My dear precious one, I am pleased with you. Your compassion has touched many a child and many an adult, and it shall continue to do so.

My dear precious one, I am pleased with you. Know ye not that I am the I Am, and in these next few days, in these next few months, you shall know and see more of what I Am really is.

I am your life. I am your all. I am your provision. I am your compassion. I am your knowledge. I am your wisdom. I am never, never late. I am always on time. And I am ready to do some mighty things in your life

Appropriate these mighty things with the words of your mouth, with your faith, and with your praise. Appropriate these things in your life. My children perish for lack of knowledge. With the knowledge that you have, I would that you gain more, and I would

153

that you'd pray for the spirit of wisdom to fall upon you so that you may have the wisdom to use the knowledge that you have.

Hold close to Me, my dear, and together let's move on. You cannot remain static. You cannot stand still. Either you're going forward or you're going backwards.

Hold on to Me. Hold on to Me, and we will ride on the winds of the high places. Like on hinds' feet, we shall jump from mountain to mountain, each one higher, higher, higher, higher, higher, higher, higher!

Love, God

THERE ARE NO LIMITATIONS

My Child:

There is no limit to the height that you can reach in the spiritual realm. I would that you could live in the high places and never, ever have to go down into the valley.

Continue on. Press on. Keep your hand to that plow, and don't look back. Don't look back. Place your hand in Mine, and don't look back.

My peace unto you, My child. My peace in you, My peace around you, My peace envelops you. My peace flows over you as waves from the ocean depositing beautiful things into your life. When the waters recede, they leave behind the sediment of enriched soil.

When the waves of peace come over you, they bring beautiful things from My Kingdom and when they recede, they leave within you My peace, My love, My riches. With every wave comes the hundredfold return.

Cast your bread upon the waters, and it shall return to you. Be eve-conscious of the peace—the peace I give to you.

When you lose the peace, then you know that Satan is launching an attack against you. Satan cannot operate where peace prevails. No, he can't! He likes disorder and confusion. He inhabits turmoil, but when My peace is there, he flees. It makes him uncomfortable.

I have said to you, My child, "My peace I give you: not as the world gives peace. But My peace is beyond understanding." Everything in you and around you functions as I created it to function when you live in an environment of peace. So that's your cue to step up your attack on the enemy of your soul, Satan.

When the peace that passes all understanding leaves, get it back. "How?" you ask. Simply by casting your cares on Me. Let Me be the burden bearer. Don't you carry any burdens! Turn to Me. Seek Me in My Word and in praise and worship. My child, you're free of cares, of burdens, of turmoil, of confusion. You prosper and are in health because you live in peace. Peace be to you, My child, now and forevermore.

Love, God

I AM THE I AM

Dearest Child:

Do you realize how big I am? Do you realize how great I am? Now that you are in My family and call Me "Friend," guard against taking Me for granted as human friends often do. Don't ever slip into thinking of Me just as your Friend.

Always remember that I am the One who scooped out the ocean beds. I am the One who flung the stars from off My fingertips. I hung the earth on nothing. I put the birds in the air and the fish in the sea—and it is by the word of My power that all of the universe is upheld and kept in motion.

When you first responded to Me and became My child, you were awed by Who I am and what I am and what I can do and what I am willing to do for you. How I longed for the day that you would develop a personal relationship with Me! And now you have!

What a thrill it is to fellowship with you!

But be on guard, My child! Don't begin to think of Me just as a Friend and forget all that I Am and all that I am capable of doing! Always remember that I am the great I Am, and I am always ready to help you.

Don't try to do things in your own strength, for I am your strength. Lean not on your own understanding. Lean on Me! Don't carry your burdens. Cast them on Me. Don't live in fear, because I have given you the truth, and I have set you free.

Don't live in poverty, for I am your Source, and I supply all of your need according to My riches in glory. Don't live in sickness and poor health, for I wish above all things that you would prosper and be in health, even as your soul prospers.

Now your soul has been prospering. Therefore, your body should be prospering too. Live the abundant life right now! You are with the redeemed. I have redeemed you from sin, sickness, and disease. My blood has washed away all of your sins. You are forgiven.

By the stripes My Son bore on His back, you are healed. Be healed now in Jesus' name.

Love, God

ABIDING IN ME

Dear Child:

"Remain in Me, and I will remain in you. No branch can bear fruit by itself; it must remain in the vine. Neither can you bear fruit unless you remain in Me" (John 15:4).

You have been grafted into the Vine; you see, I am the Vine, and I call every branch that is grafted into Me to bear fruit. If you are not bearing fruit, do not think that it is because I have cut you off. No! Remain on the Vine, even though you are not bearing fruit.

I wait patiently. I stand and wait. I know you shall produce fruit, because your heart is fixed on Me and My love.

Now you must move forward and bring life into your branches so that you may increase and multiply.

You do this by setting your feet on My Word. Stand on My Word. Stand firmly. I am the Word. Follow wherever My Word leads you, for My Words are life. My Words are life to you. My Words are life to every branch that is on the Vine. The branches will never die because they have been born again and have eternal life. However, the branches may wither and lead unproductive lives.

Oh, I call you to be an active part of the Vine, not a dormant part that produces nothing. I have empowered you by My Holy Spirit to bear fruit beyond any measure you can imagine. You have the power. My Spirit is power. Now you need the Word. My Words are life.

My child, must I keep reminding you over and over? My Words are life! My Words are life! My Words are life! You need life in you and around you. Your children and family need it.

You need My Word to dwell in you richly so that you may bear much fruit. I have left My Word to guide you, to comfort you, to teach you. I have sent the Holy Spirit to give you the power you need to use My Words. Speak My Words only. That is, release My Words, release your faith, abide in Me, let My Words abide in you.

Speak My Words! Do not waver. Set your feet firmly on My Word. I am the Word. Follow wherever My Word leads.

Speak My Words, and whatever you ask will come to pass. You see, if you abide in Me, and My words abide in you, you will be able to ask for anything, and it shall be done!

Love, God

LIVE TODAY

Dear One:

You need to let go of all of the cares of this world. You need to let go of all of the problems that you are holding on to. You think you have let go because you are not actively speaking about them, but your mind is meditating on them all the time.

Thoughts come in your mind about mistakes that you've made in the past. Do not entertain those thoughts. Push them out of your mind. You think of all the things that could go wrong in the future, and while you engage in thoughts of the past and thoughts of the future, you are not living in the present to your fullest potential. You are not utilizing that precious gift that I have given you—the gift of time.

I have exhorted you in My Word, "This is the day that the Lord has made. Let us rejoice and be glad in it." Rejoice, rejoice, and again I say, rejoice! That is not an idle comment given to My children. That is a plan of action—a plan for a life that overcomes circumstances.

Every day I give you a new day. What will you do with this day? How did you spend yesterday? How will you spend tomorrow? I am not a God of yesterday. I am not a God of tomorrow. I am a God of today! I live in the present—this very moment.

When you grasp that fact, you will not have one more unproductive day in your life.

At this moment, take heart. Do not be discouraged. Your faith is working. Yes, I know the circumstances around you do not seem like it. But you are My child, and you are not ruled by circumstances. I have set you free from circumstances.

You are a faith person, and the energy of that faith has the ability to bring into the physical realm everything that is yours in the spiritual realm. Just continue to move in love and faith according to My Word, and those circumstances around you will change. It is energized faith in My Word that brings results. Faith is the key that unlocks the storehouses of heaven.

This very day, it is possible for you and Me together to transform your wilderness into a place of success by acknowledging every good thing that is in you in Christ Jesus.

Love, God

PARTAKE OF ALL MY PROMISES

My Child!

You're living far below your potential. You could be enjoying peace in your spirit, soul, and body right now if only you would remain anchored in Me. There are so many of My promises that you are not partaking of because you allow fear and discouragement to come in your life.

Your faith is strong, resolute, and unwavering when it comes to standing and agreeing for My will in another person's life, but when anything pertains to your family, you are easily swayed by the circumstances around you

Time and time again I have told you and I remind you again, if you need healing, pray for someone else to be healed. If you have unsaved loved ones, pray that someone else will be saved. This sounds backwards to the worldly mind, but it is My way, and My ways are higher than your ways. My thoughts are higher than your thoughts.

Focus on doing for others, and this will make it easier for you to stop dwelling on the problems you are facing now in your family. When you do so, you will also be putting the law of sowing and reaping into effect. There is no way that you can give and give to others without having a harvest of blessings come to you. For whatever you sow, in due time, you shall reap if you faint not. I say, don't become weary in doing good; for eventually we shall reap a harvest, if we don't faint.

Listen to these promises:

"Come unto me, all ye that labor and are heavy laden, and I will give you rest" (Matthew 11:28).

"Cast thy bread upon the waters: for thou shalt find it after many days" (Ecclesiastes 11:1).

"My brethren, count it all joy when ye fall into divers temptations; knowing this, that the trying of your faith worketh patience" (James 1:2,3).

"Trust in the Lord, and do good; so shalt thou dwell in the land, and verily thou shalt be fed" (Psalm 37:3).

"Being confident of this very thing, that he which hath begun a good work in you will perform it until the day of Jesus Christ" (Philippians 1:6).

"And this is the confidence that we have in him, that, if we ask any thing according to his will, he heareth us. And if we know that he hear us, whatsoever we ask, we know that we have the petitions that we desired of him" (1 John 5:14,15).

Love, God

WALK IN LOVE AND IN POWER

My Precious Child!

Happy Birthday, dear one! How I remember the day you were born! It brought such joy to Me, for you see, you were exactly what I wanted. You were exactly how I had planned you to be.

I had been watching you grow and develop in your mother's womb, and I was a part of the joy both your mother and father felt at being able to cooperate with Me in bringing you into this world, a precious, unique individual, made in My image and likeness.

There is no one else like you—and I planned it that way. No one can fellowship with Me in exactly the same way that you can. No one can bring Me the same type of joy that you can bring Me. No one looks like you, talks like you, sings like you. You are you! You are what I created you to be!

I have a plan for your life. When you're in tune with it, you prosper and flourish in all areas of your life. You have sought Me, and you know what you should do, for I've revealed My will for your life in My Word. Yes, I know, child, many, many obstacles have been put in your path, but you are an overcomer. You are a winner. You win and you win big when you let Me be in charge of your life.

Have you lost sight of the truth that nothing is too hard for Me? All I need is free access in your life. All I need is for you to seek Me and live in the light of the revelations I have given you.

You don't have to let Satan win. What is it you want in your life? What is it you want in your family? Is what you want against My Word? If it isn't, then it can be yours. Have you been praying amiss? Have you bound all the things that should have been bound? Have you loosed all the things that should be loosed?

You see, child, you have authority. Use it. Be a wise steward of your time. You do things that should be the duty of others. On the surface, these things seem nice and kind to do, but they keep you from having time to fight the good fight of faith.

Strife, disharmony, backbiting, tale-bearing—all these things you have the authority to get out of your family if you will take the time to do it. Make time, child. It is a matter of life or death.

Love, God

FIGHTING SATAN FOR YOUR TIME

My Dear Child:

Fight! I say. Stand tall and fight the good fight of faith. Make time. Take time.

Delegate tasks to others so you can have time to help your family be free of Satan's oppression. Satan has deceived you into thinking you are helping them by doing things for them. Oh no, that does not help them. That hurts them, because then you don't have the time or energy to seek Me in My Word.

Build yourself up in the Word so you can do spiritual battle for your family.

I know you, My child. You love your children as much as I love you, and if even one person would come towards one of your children to harm them in any way, you would throw yourself body, soul, and spirit into the fight to save them.

Why then don't you do whatever needs to be done to throw yourself into the fight against the spiritual forces coming against them?

Oh, My child, if you could see into the spirit world, you'd go into your prayer closet and refuse to occupy your time with anything that is not your rightful duty so you would have time to fight the good fight of faith.

It is time that you rise up and defend your time—to not let anything keep you from doing what has to be done in order that your children will all come into the Kingdom and grow up to full spiritual maturity.

Do not be deceived. Not everyone who says, "Lord, Lord," will enter into the Kingdom. Salvation must be done in the heart, not just with the lips and body.

How will you know them—My children? You'll know them by their fruits. Good fruit comes from good trees.

My eye went to and fro to seek someone to help them, and I found you! Make yourself that effective instrument that I know you can be when you take the time. Begin now to intercede before it's too late, for I am coming soon.

Before you begin to intercede, start at square one. Forgive anyone and everyone, forgive yourself. You must forgive even if you do not think that you are in the wrong. You must get the strife out at whatever cost.

There are two times you should forgive: 1) When you're at fault; 2) When you're not at fault. Whatever it takes, take the first step, My child.

Love, God

FIGHTING SATAN WITH FORGIVINESS

Dear Child:

In bringing peace to your world, humble yourself to take the blame for everything if necessary. Just do the first step to getting your family in unity and harmony. Feelings don't count. You don't have to feel anything. Forgive in Jesus' name.

By not forgiving, you are holding a covering over your spouse's head and over the head of each of your children, and I cannot reach them through that covering.

Release them. Release your mate and your children so I can work in their lives.

It does not matter who is at fault. A doctor never wastes precious moments to find out who is responsible for harming a person who is wounded before he begins to patch the wounded person up. No! The doctor immediately sets out to save that person's life. In fact, that's the only purpose sometimes.

Most doctors are not even concerned with who did the wounding. They leave that to the police and others to take care of. They do their job and their job only.

This is what you should do. Don't let members of your family fix blame on who did this or that. Do not repeat bad reports, for they are a testimony to what Satan deceived someone into saying.

You are an overcomer by the blood of the Lamb and the word of your testimony of what I have done in your life.

You can be defeated by what Satan has been able to get you and others to say or do. Do you want to take the wind out of the devil's sails? It's easy. Forgive! That's step one. Nothing works in an unforgiving heart. Get the strife out. Where there is strife, you give Satan permission to kick you around.

Intercession must come out of clean vessels for it to be effective. Repent of any sins of omission and commission. Just purge yourself so you can be an effective intercessor.

I tell you, child, Satan wants your family. Are you going to allow him to have them? Be sober, be vigilant; because your adversary the devil, as a roaring lion, walks about seeking whom he may devour.

You are in a fight, and if you lose, your family will miss heaven. So make time for prayer and forgiveness. It is your lifeline to Me. It could mean your family's salvation.

Love, God

YOUR CONTRIBUTIOM
TO THE BODY OF CHRIST

My Dear Child!

Nothing is going to be too insignificant to do for the Body of Christ! Sometimes one service will be held just so one person can get saved. You are not to count the cost! You are to be attuned to My voice and obey.

What disturbs the world now? What disturbs the Body now? Is it the major problems, or the small variations in belief?

What annoys you about people? Is it their obvious bad habits and acts, or the small habits that they repeat over and over again that bring you frustration, annoyance, discouragement, and even despair?

There are no insignificant acts that any one of you can do for the Body of Christ—a look, a touch, a smile, a hug. These things can and will set people free in all areas of life.

There is no time for idle chatter. There is no time for waiting for things to happen. It isn't, "Someday I will do this for Jesus!" It is, "What I am doing right now is for Jesus, and no one but me can do it exactly like me, because there is no one else like me in the whole world. If I don't do it, it won't get done in the precise way God wants it done, for no two people do everything alike. Every little thing I do is important and necessary."

Nothing is too insignificant to do for the Body of Christ! Nothing! Let Me repeat it, nothing is too insignificant for the Body of Christ.

Every member of the Body must ask, "Lord, what is it You want me to do before You come again?" Nothing is too insignificant to do for the Body of Christ. You are to be busy doing whatever needs to be done. You are not to put off doing things.

If a baby's diaper needs changing, change it.

If a lawn needs mowing, mow it.

If dishes need to be washed, wash them.

If a letter needs to be written, write it.

Do what needs to be done in your life. Do it as unto Me.

Don't be like the servants who were found idle when their master returned. Don't be like the foolish virgins who ran out of oil in their lamps. You, My child, do whatever needs to be done to fulfill the calling I have put on your life. Prepare! Be ready, for soon things will explode in your world.

Love, God

STEP INTO NEW LIFE

Dear Beloved Child:

Weep not, but rather rejoice in Me. My ways are higher than your ways, and My ways are perfect, even for your loved one!

Trust Me to open a door that will bring great joy to your household. Trust Me. Just take a few more steps and look to Me. I am the author and finisher of your faith. I won't disappoint you.

All is well. Let My love flow through you. All is well. I am satisfied with you, for you see, I do not look upon you with natural eyes. When I see you, I see you washed as clean as snow. I look at you, and I see Jesus, for I look on the heart. And your heart is fixed on Him.

In Him you live and move and have your being. You have stepped into new life.

Have you lost patience, "abandoned" your children and grandchildren because they do not always behave in a loving way? Then what makes you think I'd abandon you when you sometimes walk out of love?

I have said, "Narrow is the way that leads to heaven." Do you know what the narrow way is? It is the Love Walk. In new life, you must stay in the Love Walk.

When you fall off the Love Walk, repent. Dust yourself off, and get on the right path again. Do it again and again. Soon you will make a rut for yourself on the path, and then you won't fall off as much.

Do you want to know how to keep confidences? Do you want to know how to keep from repeating everything you hear? Do you want to have victory in this area? You see, you need to discipline your tongue. Lack of self-discipline is the undoing of most of My children.

Listen now! Hear this! Hear Me and obey! And you shall walk in victory. Do this, My child. Before you ever share a bit of news with anyone, share it with Me. Say, "Father, isn't it great about [share your news]?" Have a conversation with Me. Then be quiet and listen to Me talk. You see, I do not offend. When you do this, you will know whom you should share things with and when you should share things. Most important of all, you will know if you should share things.

Learn to be quiet. If you must talk, talk to Me. Do not try to be a natural bridge between family members. I want you to be a spiritual bridge in prayer—in secret—not in constant talking.

Love, God

PRESSING FORWARD IN CHRIST

Dear One:

My dear child, I want you to forget all the things that are behind you and press on toward the mark that is the high calling of Jesus Christ.

Let the words of your mouth be My words. Fresh water and salt water do not come out of the same stream. My love has been shed abroad in your heart and that love is perfecting you more and more into My image.

My love shines forth from you in your smile, in your eyes, in your actions. Love shines from you because love is in you. Oh, My dear child! My precious child! How I love you! I love you so much that I died on the cross for you. I endured all sin and all diseases so that you would not have to bear them.

I bore all your griefs so that you wouldn't have to bear any. So, why do you carry around with you the cares of this world? They are not yours to carry. Give them to Me. Cast all of your cares on Me. Trust in Me and do good. Delight yourself in Me. Commit your way unto Me. Trust Me, and I will help you.

My dear, I want you to know that I am pleased with you. You are the apple of My eye. I continually encompass you about with mercy and loving-kindness. I intercede for you daily. I know the circumstances that you're in right now. I know that Satan has been shooting fiery darts at you from every side. I know that he is battling you in your mind. He puts thoughts in your mind.

Don't listen to Satan. He prowls around like a hungry, roaring lion, looking for someone to devour. But he cannot devour you! No! No! No! For you are God's property!

You have been bought with a price! You are made free from sin! You cannot be defeated!

You are a winner! You are redeemed from the curse. You are more than a conqueror. You're redeemed from darkness.

You are a child of light. You're redeemed from poverty. Your needs are met according to His riches in glory. You're redeemed from sickness and disease. By His stripes you are healed!

You are redeemed from loneliness and depression. The joy of the Lord is your strength. You're redeemed from family problems and friend problems. The love of God has been shed abroad in your heart, and that love fills the empty void that used to be in your heart.

Love, God

IMITATORS OF CHRIST

Dear Child:

I sincerely want you to imitate Me. I want you to be perfect as I am perfect! You have put your hand to the plow, now don't turn back. Don't look to the right nor to the left. Keep you eyes on Me! I will lead you to the high places. Together we shall go on from glory to glory.

No mountain can stand in your way because you have the authority to say to it, "Be removed!" You will be glorifying My Son's name when you do it! Let My Word abide in you. Then whatsoever you ask in Jesus' name, I will hasten to perform it.

When you speak My Words, you commission the angels to work in your behalf. They are working for you now.

I want you to always remember that you are loved. I love you, dear, I love you so very, very much. I gave My life for you so that you could be translated from the kingdom of darkness into the Kingdom of light.

That light in you is Me. Let your light shine for the whole world to see. Let people know you are a Christian by the light and love that shine forth from you. I need your help because so many of My children are walking in darkness.

Let your light shine so you can show them the way to eternal life with Me in heaven!

Love lifts! Love heals! Love endures! Love never fails! Let the love that has been shed abroad in your heart shine forth in all its glory, and love will show you the path where you should go. Love will point out the right road for you to walk. Love will lead you, teach you, protect you.

Love is the greatest power operating in you right now, and that love is Me! Because I am love. Through My eyes of love, look around and see people doing the ordinary things of life. You'll see them chatting, buying groceries, involved just as you are.

You witness a mother pushing her child in a stroller and you wonder, "How can she be so unconcerned when I am hurting so much?" My child, I understand. Come, walk with Me in your hour of need.

Come, talk with me about the difficult situations in your life. I know how you feel. Oh, yes I do! For you see, I have experienced all of your sorrows. I have sat in your place. I know all about it. As you understand this, something good is going to happen to you.

Love, God

I WILL REWARD YOU

Dearest One:

Yes, I know how you are feeling right now at this moment! It seems that you labor and labor without reward. No one seems to notice what you do or how well you do it. Do not look to other people—look to Me! It really doesn't matter what people think about you. What matters is what I think about you.

You are an excellent person filled with the power and might of My Word, well equipped to preach and teach the gospel in season and out of season. You are a reservoir of revelation knowledge just waiting to be poured out on fertile fields. Do not despair. Do not allow discouragement to come in. Discouragement is not from Me!

You hold the key to unlock every door that is barred. You have Jesus' name, and you have faith in His name. Whatever you ask Me for in the name of Jesus, I will give it to you!

I have decreed that Jesus' name is above every name in heaven, on earth, and under the earth. There is no other name greater than the name of Jesus. What is in your life that needs to be bound right now? Bind it in the name of Jesus. What is in your life that needs to be loosed right now? Loose it in the name of Jesus. Use His name. It's the key that will unlock every door for you.

Jesus' name belongs to you. You have the authority to use His name. Begin to use it daily in your life. Victory is yours—just receive it in the name of Jesus! Remember that at the sound of His name every knee shall bow.

In the name of Jesus, you can be free from oppression. Oppression, bow your knee. In the name of Jesus, you can be free from lack. Lack has no place in your life. In the name of Jesus you can be free—free to be what I have called you to be.

I have set a path before you that leads to victory in all areas of your life. The path has been long and troubled. Yet you have overcome every obstacle that Satan has put in your way.

As long as you're in the world, Satan will shoot fiery darts at you to get you off the path that I have set you upon. But you shall overcome. Victory is yours always.

Use the weapons I have given you. Use Jesus' name. And you will defeat Satan every time. In the name of Jesus, you are totally free!

Love, God

ENCOURAGEMENT

My Dear Child:

You've run the course I've set before you. You've finished every race that I have ever called you to enter—and you've always run well! Everything you have ever done for Me has been first class.

You have always been concerned with the way My image is presented to the world. I want you to know that I appreciate that very much. I appreciate the fact that you not only set out to do things for Me—but you do them lovingly and you do them well.

You always put Me first. I have observed all the times and all the ways that people have risen up against you. I have seen and heard their accusations, insults, putdowns, and teasing over your decisions to do what I've called you to do. I marvel at your confidence in that you have heard Me.

I am impressed, too, with your single-eyed tenacity in doing what I have called you to do.

I present a project to you. You hear Me; you settle it in your heart exactly what it is I want you to do; then you set out to obey Me. From that point on, you confer with no one.

Like My Son, when He came down from the mountain and faced Jerusalem and certain death, You are able to set your face like flint and nothing deters you from accomplishing the task at hand. Whatever the task, in Jesus' name, you see it through to completion. Thank you.

My child, be encouraged! Take heart! Lift up your eyes and look to the fields. Now is the time for the fulfillment of the visions and dreams I have given you. It is time for harvest. It is time to reap. Everything is set.

I have opened the door—walk on through. Don't let go of your dreams and the vision I've given you, for this is the season of fruition.

I love you, My child. I am so pleased that you are My child. You have always willingly obeyed Me in whatever I've asked you to do for the Body of Christ. You have put Me and others before yourself. You have found the balance between Me, family, and friends.

And most important of all, you have always walked worthy of Me. You have not made Me ashamed! You have represented Me well. Thank you, child! Thank you!

Love, God

USE YOUR AUTHORITY

My Dear:

You go up and down and all around. You search here and there and everywhere. You look for something, you know not what. You just know that there's more to life than this. You sink lower and lower, almost into despair, until finally you realize that I am still there.

I've been waiting all along, for you to come back to Me where you belong.

Child, why do you stray and nearly go completely away from Me before you recognize the games that the devil plays? He has no new tricks, that's for sure. All he ever does is play a tune in your head that puts you down and sometimes makes you wish you were dead.

He'd like that, you know, if you weren't here. But, oh! How dreadful that would be for Me. Sure, I'd be happy to have you here in heaven with all your loved ones and Me. But tell Me, where could I find someone else to do the work that you do? Who would be faithful to love and to pray, for each and every person that I send your way?

You think your life is useless when you look around and see all the strife that still can be found. But what would life be like in your family and town if you had never been around? Things may seem dreary now to you. But without you, I tell you, that town where you live would be a terrible place to be if you weren't there. For you are My ambassador whom I have sent forth, to bring in the harvest with force.

You see, that's where you miss it sometimes, My beloved. You still don't use force on the one who offends. Certainly I have given you all things that you need to live and to learn and do every deed. But you must enforce it on earth, don't you see? For it's to you that I have given the authority.

So learn every promise and command in My book, and appropriate them for yourself and anyone Satan is trying to hook. I'll not leave you defenseless, that's for sure. You still have My Word, Jesus' Name, and His blood. Now you use those weapons so that you will win every battle the devil engages you in.

There is no other way to win. No, there just isn't. For as long as you remain on earth, you'll have the devil to fight, so get it over quickly with force and with might.

Love, God

YOUR CHILDREN ARE MINE

Dearest Child:

My child! My child! Why do you fret? There is nothing man can do to you that can harm you. I am for you. I am on your side. My grace has been abounding in the lives of all of your children. I've chosen each one for a work, and My grace is present for them to be able to accomplish that work.

I'm holding your child in the palm of My hand. I am tenderly stripping all of the outer worldly trappings off of him. You think you know him, but you will be surprised when you see him as he really is. His spirit is gentle. He is meek, and My word says that the meek shall inherit the earth.

The fellowship your son needed after he became a new creation has been following him around, and it will catch up with him soon. The fellowship he needs is available now, and you will be astounded at how fast it will come to pass in his life. I will rekindle in his heart the desire to read My Word that he had when he first became born again.

And this time, the right people will be around to fellowship with him and feed him the meat of the Word. He will grow up in Me. He shall be a witness for Me, not only because of what he said, but because of who he is. People will be able to look at him and see Me, for he is made in My image, and I am forming him into My likeness more and more each day.

You have trained up your child in the way he should go, and he will not depart from that training. I tell other parents, stand your ground! Don't give up! The devil would just love to get you to quit!

Don't give up on your child. You're not a quitter. You're a winner! Keep on! Press in. Keep on applying prayer. Do not be weary in well-doing, for in due season you shall reap the harvest of blessing you have been believing for if you refuse to quit.

Victory for sons and daughters is at hand. Victory is right around the corner. How can you know? Why, haven't you noticed that the devil always fights the hardest just before you receive your answer? That's his last big effort to get you to become weary and faint. But you won't faint. I give you the victory!

Love, God

NO SMALL THINGS WITH GOD

My Dearest:

Count it no small thing when you give a book to a friend. Count it no small thing! Count it no small thing when you give a word of encouragement, when you give a smile, when you write a short note to someone, or when you visit a friend. Count it no small thing!

For you see, there is no such thing as a smallness in the Kingdom of God. Count it no small thing when you love the unlovely, for that is the beginning of making them lovely. The reason people act unlovely is because they do not feel loved.

Just as a loved person can be hurt and beat down by rejecting him and withholding love, so can an unloved person be healed and lifted up by giving him love.

Love—that's the key! You keep thinking that you are not ready to do My Work, that you are not prepared, but you are prepared. I have not called you to be a preacher or a teacher. No, I have simply called you to love.

"Beloved, let us love one another: for love is of God; and every one that loveth is born of God. He that loveth not knoweth not God; for God is love" (1 John 4:78).

Because I love you so, I say, look up! See those waves coming towards you! There's a blessing on each one of them for you! Now you have given. You have given of your time, your love, and your finances. You have sowed good seed, and it has produced. Look! Keep on looking, because the harvest is ready. Your harvest of blessing is ready.

Tares and weeds are small things—but beware of them in your garden. Satan would have you think you have no blessings. He has sowed weeds in your garden. He thinks the weeds will hide your blessings and discourage you. Be not dismayed. My child, be not dismayed, for I have prepared a table for you before your enemies. Right now—here on earth, My table is ready. Come and feast! I have prepared it for you. Come boldly expecting, and you will obtain.

This is your season to reap your harvest—large or small. Remember, nothing is small in My eyes. Keep on sowing, more harvest will come for you to reap.

Love, God

STEADFASTNESS

My Child, My Child:

On Christ the solid rock you stand and stand and stand and stand! Straight and tall you stand, with the winds of indecision blowing around your head and the waves of adversity lapping at your feet. Still, you stand.

Satan has tried his best to get you off of that solid Rock—off of the Word of God—but he cannot do it, and he will not do it. For you see, I am on your side. And if I be for you, who can be against you and win? Not one single person!

Child, you and I are a majority. All you have to do is be in agreement with Me and My Word. Believe My Word and stand and stand and stand! I need your unwavering faith to be manifested and solidified in quiet patience. I need your obedience. This creates an atmosphere for miracles to happen. Miracles are coming your way every day. Expect them. Receive them. Above all, don't give up!

The universal characteristic that is observed in great men and women is that they don't give up. Regardless of the odds or public opinion or how they feel or any other thing, they just keep going on. The issue is commitment to what they believe is important.

It matters not how many times you've failed. It matters not how many mistakes you've made, how many battles you've lost. What counts is if you consistently work toward reaching the goal that I have set before you.

My eyes go to and fro across the whole earth, looking for people who are wholeheartedly committed to Me and to My Word. And, I have found such a one in you. Always know that as you wholeheartedly seek Me and My will, you give Me an avenue that enables Me to show Myself strong in your behalf. This is part of your witness to your world.

There is no limit to the amount of power and resources I will use to help you. I am available. All you have to do is tap into My strength and power with your faith.

For truly miracles happen to them who trust and obey. These are the true believers.

Love, God

LEARNING TO RECEIVE

My Child:

It is your inability to receive that stops My principles from working. You yourself have been thwarting the very principles that can free you from your dilemma.

Your inability to receive has stunted your ministry of giving. You want to give, but you don't have anything to give. I have sent people to provide seed for you to sow, and you have not received it.

Therefore, you have not had seed for sowing. Because you have not sowed, you have not reaped. Because you have never reaped, you have not had anything to sow. This is an area that needs correcting in your life, not only where finances are concerned, but where forgiveness, love, comfort, and prayers are concerned.

You are so willing to forgive others. Yet, so often you do not receive forgiveness from others. Sometimes you do not receive forgiveness from Me. How, child, how can you give what you do not possess? How can you give forgiveness to others when you have not received forgiveness from Me, either directly from Me or from Me through others?

What is it that is holding you back? Why are you always so willing to pray for others, but you are not willing to accept prayers from others? Why are you not free to receive and accept gifts? Tell Me, child. Tell Me now, not because I need to know what is holding you back, but because you need to confess what is holding you back.

Child, command fear to leave in Jesus' name. Get rid of the fear of exposing your needs and your weaknesses to others. You must risk being vulnerable. You must risk sharing yourself with others, for unless you give of yourself—your love, your tenderness, your innermost thoughts—you will never be able to receive the close companionship that you desire.

Yes, I know you have attempted to do that many times in the past, and it has blown up in your face. People have used confidences you have shared with them to harm you.

Child, the answer isn't to turn inward and refuse to share yourself with anyone. The answer is to share with a trusted friend. Share with Me. I know all, and I understand all, and I want so much to help you. But you must do your part. You must confess. Confess with your mouth. When you do so, you will set a law into motion that will free you.

Turn to Me, child. Confide in Me. I will give you rest and peace.

Love, God

A NOTE TO THE READER

The family of late author Bonnie Schluter was instrumental in getting these letters published. Her son, Dr. Marc Schluter, had the letters typed and bound together, in honor of his mother's lifelong dream to have the work published. Another son, Dr. Eric Schluter, "happened" to meet a patient who works for Honor Books. A series of events fell into place and brought you this book.

We hope that *Love Letters from God* has encouraged you to draw near to God and to experience His love and grace. Bonnie Schluter's husband, Robert Schluter, selected the following letter as a loving tribute to his wife: "It so perfectly describes her and how she lived her life for her Lord."

A LOVE LETTER FROM GOD

In Memory of Bonnie Schluter

Dearest One:

How I love you! I call you blessed. I call you child. I call you friend. I call you co-laborer with Me in bringing souls into the Kingdom.

The absence of light brings darkness. My child! My child! Don't you realize that your absence brings gloom in the lives of many around you? You have often wondered, "Why am I here, Lord? Why am I surrounded by people who do not lift me up? Why, Lord?"

Don't you see, child, that I do not have enough children who operate in the gift of joy? I do not have enough children who, like you, unselfishly put others before themselves, without thought of what they are receiving in return.

Child! When you walk into a room, gloom disperses, depression flees, for you are a ray of sunshine in the lives of many. You bring light and love and joy wherever you go.

You do not put on love. You do not purpose in your heart to go out and love people. You just do it naturally because love is

195

in you. Just as effortlessly as you breathe in oxygen and exhale carbon dioxide, you breathe in the Holy Spirit and exhale love. You breathe in God and exhale praise. Praise is forever on your lips.

I have seen you. I have watched you sow seeds of love and praise in rocky fields. You have tilled the soil in the lives of many. You have removed the rocks in their lives—the hurts, depressions, and self-pity. Yes, you have, child. You do it so effortlessly that joy is yours. Others may want to be like you, but they don't know how. Yet, just your presence helps people.

Yes, I know there are times when you do not feel joyful, but you really aren't aware of the effect your presence has on people. You become so much a part of their lives that they cannot even comprehend how dull and lifeless their lives would be without you.

You are a sower of peace. You are a sower of joy, comfort, and patience. You are that fruitful branch that draws from the Vine.

You are not aware of how much you contribute to the well-being and happiness of others. That is why I am telling you today, you are a very special part of the Body of Christ and though the enemy comes against you in all directions, fear not, for I am with you.

Love, God